FLASHMAPS
WASHINGTON DC

Editor
Robert Blake

Creative Director
Fabrizio La Rocca

Cartographer
David Lindroth

Designer
Tigist Getachew

Editorial Updater
Joseph Rio

Cartographic Updater
Marcy Pritchard

Editorial Contributor
Martha Schulman

Cartographic Contributors
Edward Faherty
Sheila Levin
Page Lindroth
Eric Rudolph

Contents

Special Sales

Fodor's Travel Publications are available at special discounts for bulk purchases for sales promotions or premiums. Special editions, including personalized covers, excerpts of existing guides, and corporate imprints, can be created in large quantities for special needs. For more information, contact your local bookseller or write to Special Markets, Fodor's Travel Publications, 201 East 50th St., New York, NY 10022. Inquiries from Canada should be directed to your local Canadian bookseller or sent to Random House of Canada, Ltd., Marketing Dept., 2775 Matheson Blvd. E.,Mississauga, Ontario L4W 4P7. Inquiries from the United Kingdom should be sent to Fodor's Travel Publications, 20 Vauxhall Bridge Rd., London, England SW1V 2SA. **ISBN 0-679-00223-5**

PRINTED IN THE UNITED STATES OF AMERICA 10 9 8 7 6 5 4 3 2 1

Area Codes: DC (202); Maryland (301), (410); Virginia (703). All (202) unless otherwise noted.

EMERGENCIES

Ambulance, Fire, Police ☎ 911

AAA Emergency Road Service ☎ 703/222-5000

Adult Protective Services ☎ 727-2345

AMEX Lost Travelers Checks ☎ 800/221-7282

Animal Bites ☎ 576-6665

Animal Clinic ☎ 363-7300

Battered Women ☎ 347-2777

Children's Protection ☎ 727-0995

Deaf Emergency ☎ 727-9334

Dentist/Doctor Referral ☎ 362-8677

Drug/Alcohol Hotline ☎ 800/821-4357

Hazardous Wastes ☎ 645-6080

Poison Control ☎ 625-3333

Police (non-emergency) ☎ 727-1010

Psychiatric Response ☎ 727-0739

Rape & Assault ☎ 333-7273

Suicide Prevention ☎ 727-0700

US Park Police ☎ 619-7300

SERVICES

AAA ☎ 703/222-6000

AIDS Hotline ☎ 332-2437

Alcoholics Anonymous ☎ 966-9115

American Red Cross ☎ 728-6400

Better Business Bureau ☎ 393-8000

Chamber of Commerce ☎ 347-7201

Crime Solvers ☎ 393-2222

DC Government ☎ 727-1000

Dept of Aging ☎ 724-5626

Federal Information ☎ 647-4000

Food Stamps ☎ 727-0858

Foreign Exchange Rates ☎ 800/287-7362

Human Services ☎ 279-6000

Immigration ☎ 800/755-0777

Legal Aid Society ☎ 628-1161

Mayor's Office ☎ 727-2980

Medicaid ☎ 724-5173

Medicare ☎ 800/638-6833

Motor Vehicle Information ☎ 727-6680

Passport Office ☎ 647-0518

Planned Parenthood ☎ 347-8500

Salvation Army ☎ 546-3130

Sanitation ☎ 727-4825

Social Security ☎ 800/772-1213

Supreme Court ☎ 479-3000

Time of Day ☎ 703/844-2525

Transportation for Handicapped ☎ 462-8658

US Capitol ☎ 224-3121

US Coast Guard ☎ 267-2229

US Customs Services ☎ 927-6724

US Internal Revenue ☎ 800/829-1040

US Postal Service ☎ 682-9595

Virginia Travel Center ☎ 659-5523

Visitor Information ☎ 347-2873

Washington Convention & Visitors Association ☎ 789-1600

Washington DC Accommodations ☎ 289-2220; 800/554-2220

Weather ☎ 703/936-1212

YMCA ☎ 232-6700

YWCA ☎ 626-0700

TRANSPORTATION

Airport Connection ☎ 301/441-2345

Amtrak ☎ 484-7540

Amtrak Metroliner Service ☎ 800/872-7245

Amtrak Package Express Service ☎ 906-3125

Baltimore-Washington International Airport ☎ 800/435-9294

Capitol Cab ☎ 546-2400

Diamond Cab ☎ 387-6200

Dulles International Airport ☎ 703/572-7200

Greyhound Bus Information ☎ 800/231-2222

Marc-Camden Line Commuter ☎ 800/325-7245

Marc-Penn Line Commuter ☎ 800/325-7245

Metrobus & Metrorail Transit Information ☎ 637-7000; 638-3780

Reagan Nat'l Airport ☎ 703/417-8000

Union Station Information ☎ 371-9441

Virginia Railway Express ☎ 703/658-6200

Washington Flyer ☎ 703/685-1400

Yellow Cab ☎ 544-1212

Area Codes: DC (202); Maryland (301), (410); Virginia (703). All (202) unless otherwise noted.

TOURS

Black History National Recreation Trail ☎ 208-4747

C&O Barge Trips ☎ 301/299-2026

Construction Watch and Site Seeing ☎ 272-2448

Dandy Cruises ☎ 703/683-6076

FBI Tour ☎ 324-2892

Goodwill Embassy Tours ☎ 636-4225

Gray Line Tours ☎ 289-1995

National Cathedral ☎ 537-6200

Old Town Trolley Tours ☎ 301/985-3021

Pentagon Tour ☎ 703/695-1776

Scandal Tours ☎ 783-7212

Smithsonian Resident Associate Program ☎ 357-3030

Spirit of Mount Vernon ☎ 554-8000

Spirit of Washington ☎ 554-8000

Tourmobile ☎ 554-7950

Washington Post ☎ 334-7969

White House Tours ☎ 456-7041

PARKS AND RECREATION

Arlington National Cemetery ☎ 703/697-2131

Baltimore Ravens ☎ 888/919-9797

Canoe Cruisers Hotline ☎ 301/656-2586

Cherry Blossom Festival ☎ 728-1137

C&O Canal Park Service ☎ 653-5190

Cooke Stadium ☎ 301/276-6000

Cycling ☎ 628-2500

DC Armory ☎ 547-9077

DC Parks & Recreation ☎ 673-7660

Dial-A-Park ☎ 619-7275

East Potomac Park ☎ 485-9880

Great Falls Visitor Center ☎ 703/285-2966

Laurel Race Park ☎ 301/725-0400

MCI Center ☎ 628-3200

National Aquarium ☎ 482-2825

National Arboretum ☎ 245-2726

National Botanical Garden ☎ 225-8333

National Park Service ☎ 619-7222

National Zoo ☎ 673-4800

Oriole Park at Camden Yards ☎ 410/685-9800

Patriot Center ☎ 703/993-3000

Road Runners Club ☎ 703/836-0558

RFK Stadium ☎ 547-9077

Rock Creek Park ☎ 282-1063

Rosecroft Raceway ☎ 301/567-4000

Tennis Information ☎ 673-7646

US Airways Arena ☎ 301/350-3400

Washington Capitals ☎ 301/336-2277

Washington Mystics ☎ 661-5000

Washington Redskins ☎ 301/276-6000

Washington Wizards ☎ 301/622-3865

Wolf Trap Farm Park ☎ 703/255-1800

ENTERTAINMENT

Arena Stage ☎ 488-3300

Barns at Wolf Trap Park ☎ 703/255-1868

Choral Arts Society ☎ 244-3669

Constitution Hall ☎ 638-2661

Dial-A-Movie ☎ 333-3456

Dial-A-Museum ☎ 357-2020

Ford's Theatre ☎ 426-6924

Kennedy Center ☎ 467-4600

Lansburgh Shakespeare Theatre ☎ 393-2700

Lincoln Theater ☎ 328-6000

Lisner Auditorium ☎ 994-6800

Nat'l Symphony Orchestra ☎ 416-8100

National Theatre ☎ 783-3372

Nissan Pavillon ☎ 703/754-6400

Old Post Office Pavilion Ticket Place ☎ 842-5387

Smithsonian Information ☎ 357-2700

Studio Theatre ☎ 332-3300

Ticketmaster ☎ 432-7328

Warner Theater ☎ 783-4000

Washington Ballet ☎ 362-3606

Washington Opera ☎ 800/87-OPERA

Wolf Trap ☎ 703/255-1800

SALES TAX

Washington, D.C.: 5.75%

Maryland: 5%

Virginia: 4.5%

PENNSYLVANIA

M A R Y [LAND]

Gettysburg
Battlefield
Park

76

81

Antietam
Battlefield
Park

70

Frederick

70

522

Martinsburg

Harper's
Ferry

270

Romney

50

Augusta

Winchester

Rockville

Berryville

50

495

WEST
VIRGINIA

Strausburg

Woodstock

81

Front
Royal

66

Manassas
Battlefield
Park

Arlington

Edinburg

Alexandria

Mt. Jackson

Shenandoah
Nat'l Park

29

Woodbridge
Dale City

Indian
Head

Luray

33

Stanley

Culpeper

Falmouth

Harrisonburg

Elkton

Spotsylvania
Nat'l Military Park

301

Fredericksburg

17

Staunton

Gordonsville

64

Waynesboro

Charlottesville

95

Bowling
Green

81

33

64

VIRGINIA

Appalachian Trail

29

Gum
Spring

Ashland

Aylett

Buena Vista

60

Colleen

64

295

360

Amherst

Dillwyn

Richmond

60

Bon Air

Lynchburg

Appomattox
Courthouse
Nat'l Hist. Park

95

Appomattox

Sherwood
Forest

460

Farmville

Hopewell

Brookneal

360

Burkeville

460

Colonial Heights

Petersburg
Nat'l
Battlefield

Victoria

Blackstone

Petersburg

Waverly

Kenbridge

85

Wakefield

Chatham

South Boston

Lawrenceville

29

Danville

58

360

Kerr
Reservoir

Lake
Gaston

58

Emporia

95

58

Oxford

Henderson

Roanoke
Rapids

N O R T H

85

Harrisburg
76
Lancaster
Trenton
95

York
Philadelphia
Camden
95
Wilmington
295
NEW JERSEY
83
95
L A N D
Aberdeen
13
Towson
Atlantic City
695
Baltimore
70
Chestertown
95
Glen Burnie
301
Dover
Laurel
Centreville
1
Annapolis
404
Cape May
Washington, D.C.
DELAWARE
50
Tracy's Landing
Rehoboth Beach
5
Georgetown
Waldorf
Cambridge
13
5
Prince Frederick
50
Leonardtown
Salisbury
Ocean City
Lexington Park
MARYLAND
235
Pocomoke City
Assateague Island
Warsaw
Lottsburg
Chincoteague Nat'l Seashore
Tappahannock
Burgess
Sharps
13
Kilmarnock
Onancock
Exmore
West Point
33
VIRGINIA
17
64
Williamsburg
Colonial Williamsburg
Busch Gardens
Yorktown
Yorktown Battlefield
Cape Charles
Hampton
Chesapeake Bay Bridge-Tunnel
Newport News
Cape Henry
460
Norfolk
Virginia Beach
64
Portsmouth
Chesapeake
Suffolk
Franklin
168
Dismal Swamp
Mackay Island Nat'l Wildlife Refuge
Elizabeth City
C A R O L I N A
Duck

Chesapeake Bay

ATLANTIC OCEAN

N

50 miles
0
0
75 km

Washington DC/Baltimore Corridor

MAP 2

(140) (30)

Reisterstown

Cockeysville

(140)

83

Timonium

Owings Mills

Lutherville

95

795

1

140 Baltimore Beltway

Towson

695

Joppatowne

Randallstown

83

Perry Hall

Pikesville

Parkville

40

Patapsco Valley State Park

140

70

695

26

BALTIMORE

Essex

Pine Orchard

Dundalk

Oriole Park at Camden Yards

695

Hart-Miller Pleasure Island

Ellicott City

Catonsville

95

Sparrows Point

Jonestown

895

Patapsco River

Ft. Howard

Columbia

195

175 108

Guilford

Waterloo

295

Glen Burnie

29

10

Scaggsville

Baltimore-Washington International Airport

Harundale

32

Jessup

175

3

695

1

Savage

Severn

2

100

Lake Shore

177

Odenton

32

Pasadena

95

Laurel

Fort George G. Meade

Gambrills

Severna Park

Gibson Island

Arnold

Sandy Point State Park

Beltsville

Millersville

Nat'l Agricultural Research Center

3

97

178

Severn River

College Park

Crofton

U.S. Naval Academy

50 301

Greenbelt

193

Bowie

50 301

Parole

ANNAPOLIS

704

Davidsonville

Riva

South River

Bay Ridge

Largo

Hall

Londontowne

Kent Island

214

2

Seat Pleasant

Birdsville

Mayo

Suitland

Landover

468

Shady Side

4

Forestville

301

Harwood

95

Upper Marlboro

Drury

Greenock

Churchton

Andrews Air Force Base

Bristol

Poplar Island

Mellwood

Tracys Landing

Clinton

Patuxent River Park

4

North Beach

5

Cheltenham

Naylor

Chaneyville

Chesapeake Bay

Brandywine

382

Chesapeake Beach

381

301

Cedarville State Forest

Sunderland

Waldorf

Patapsco River

Chesapeake Bay

N

0 5 miles
0 5 km

MARYLAND

270
495

University Blvd.
Georgia Ave.
Kensington
189
River Rd.
Falls Rd.
Persimmon Tree Rd.
190
Bradley Blvd.
191
Wilson La.
Bradley Blvd.
187
Wisconsin Ave.
185
355
Connecticut Ave.
Bethesda
Glen Echo
MacArthur Blvd.
Goldsboro Rd.
Somerset
Chevy Chase
Bradley La.
Beach Dr.
Oregon Ave.
Utah Ave.
Cabin John Br.
Potomac River
River Rd.
396
Military Rd.
Rock Creek Park
16th St.
193
495
Georgetown Pike
Langley
George Washington Memorial Pkwy.
MARYLAND
DISTRICT OF COLUMBIA
Wisconsin Ave.
Connecticut Ave.
National Zoological Park
Dulles
Dolley Madison Blvd.
McLean
Old Dominion Dr.
267
Maple Ave.
Dulles Airport Access Rd.
Westmoreland St.
Kirby Rd.
N. Glebe Rd.
Glebe Rd.
Military Rd.
Massachusetts Ave.
MacArthur Blvd.
Canal Rd.
C&O Canal
Calvert St.
ysons corner
New Hampshire Ave.
Gallows Rd.
Curtis Memorial Pkwy.
Williamsburg Blvd.
Lee Hwy.
Lee Hwy.
Roosevelt Island
MN
MS
Leesburg Pike
29
Washington Blvd.
Lee Hwy.
Falls Church
66
Wilson Blvd.
Arlington National Cemetery
Capital Beltway
495
Lee Hwy.
7
Arlington Blvd.
50
Leesburg Pike
Arlington Blvd.
Arlington
George Mason Dr.
Columbia Pike
Sleepy Hollow Rd.
Annandale Rd.
Gallows Rd.
Hummer Rd.
Columbia Pike
VIRGINIA
Seminary Rd.
King St.
Henry G. Shirley Memorial Hwy.
Quaker Ln.
Glebe Rd.
Mt. Vernon Ave.
Jefferson Davis Hwy.
George Washington Memorial Pkwy.
Annandale
236
Little River Tnpk.
395
Van Dorn St.
Braddock Rd.
King St.
Alexandria
1
Backlick Rd.
Braddock Rd.
Duke St.
7
236
95
Henry G. Shirley Memorial Hwy.
Capital Beltway
495
617
95
Franconia Rd.
1
ld Keene Mill Rd.
Backlick Rd.
Beulah St.
Telegraph Rd.
South Kings Hwy.
Richmond Hwy.
Fort Hunt Rd.
Hooes Rd.
1

University

Powder Mill Rd.

Beaver Dam Rd.

1

Capital Beltway

Powder Mill Rd.

Blvd.

Cherry Hill Rd.

Baltimore Ave.

Greenbelt

Adelphi Rd.

Greenbelt Rd.

Silver Spring

193

Riggs Rd.

Piney Branch Rd.

University

College Park

201

Greenbelt National Park

193

Takoma Park

650

Calvert Rd.

Kenilworth Ave.

New Carrollton

95

Lanham-Severn Rd.

Georgia Ave.

Missouri Ave.

DISTRICT OF COLUMBIA

Riggs Rd.

Ager Rd.

East West Hwy.

Adelphi Rd.

1

Riverdale Rd.

Capital Beltway

New Hampshire Ave.

15th St.

Queens Chapel Rd.

M A R Y L A N D

Washington Pkwy.

Hyattsville

Landover

◄ **NW** ► **NE**

Michigan Ave.

Kenilworth Ave.

Baltimore Ave.

Annapolis Rd.

202

Irving St.

Columbia Rd.

29

Rhode Island Ave.

Bladensburg Rd.

Landover Rd.

Cheverly

Martin Luther King Jr. Hwy.

US Airways Arena/ Cooke Stadium

Capital Beltway

U St.

N. Capital St.

1

New York Ave.

50

Massachusetts Ave.

6th St.

Florida Ave.

Sheriff Rd.

Hill Rd.

MCI Center

Maryland Ave.

Benning Rd.

704

Constitution Ave.

US Capitol

11th St.

◄ **NE** ►

E. Capitol St.

Independence Ave.

6th St.

◄ **SE** ►

214

395

S. Capital St.

RFK Stadium

Capitol Heights

Ritchie Rd.

River

Massachusetts Ave.

Pennsylvania

Ritchie Rd.

Anacostia

295

Suitland Pkwy.

Ave.

Marlboro Pike

District Heights

Reagan National Airport

Alabama Ave.

Suitland Rd.

DISTRICT OF COLUMBIA

4

Forestville Rd.

Capital Beltway

◄ **SW** ► **SE**

S. Capital St.

MARYLAND

Silver Hill Rd.

Suitland Pkwy.

Bolling Air Force Base

Iverson St.

5

Morningside

Allentown Rd.

Forest Heights

Wheeler Rd.

St. Barnabas Rd.

95

Branch Ave.

Temple Hill Rd.

Andrews Air Force Base

Power House Rd.

Woodrow Wilson Br.

Capital Beltway

Brinkley Rd.

223

Indian Head Hwy.

210

Oxon Hill Rd.

Bock Rd.

Tucker Rd.

Rd.

Kirby Rd.

5

Palmer Rd.

Allentown Rd.

0   2 miles

0   3 km

N

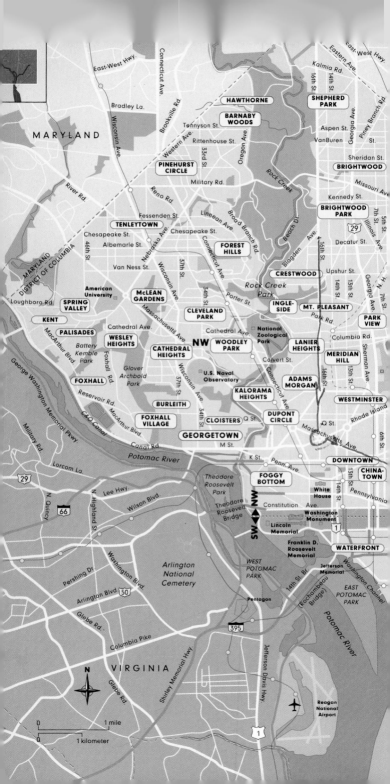

A B C

Hobart St.
Harvard St.
34th St.
34th Pl.
Cleveland Ave.
28th St.
27th St.
Woodley Rd.
Woodley Pl.
Hawthorne Ave.
Ontario Rd.
Lanier Pl.
Columbia Rd.
Calvert St.
Washington Marriott
29th St.
29th St.
McGill Terr.
28th St.
Wood land
Calvert St.
Woodley Pl.
Woodhorn Pl.
Rock Creek
Calvert St.
Shoreham
Euclid St.
17th St.
Ontario
Champlain St.
Kalorama Rd.
Biltmore St.
Mintwood Rd.
Calvert St.
Observatory La.
Naval Observatory
Normanstone Park
Normanstone Dr.
Edgevale Terr.
Benton St.
Rock Creek & Potomac Pkwy.
Kalorama Circle
Kalorama Rd.
Belmont St.
Belmont Rd.

1

W. Pl.
Observatory Circle
Massachusetts Ave.
Whitehaven St.
Waterside Dr.
Tracy Pl.
23rd St.
Wyoming Ave.
Wyoming Ave.
Columbia Rd.
California St.
Vernon St.
Seaton Pl.
Seaton St.
Willard St.
Crescent Pl.

Whitehaven Pkwy.
35th Pl.
Dumbarton Oaks Park
California
Bancroft Pl.
24th St.
Bancroft Pl.
Woodrow Wilson House
S St.
Florida Ave.
T St.
Swann St.
New Hampshire Ave.
Riggs Pl.
Riggs St.

T St. Pl.
36th St.
S St.
R St.
Montrose Park
Oak Hill Cemetery
R St.
Avon Pl.
Decatur Pl.
R St.
Sheridan Circle
Massachusetts Ave.
Q St.
19th St.
18th St.
17th St.
Church St.
P St.

2

Reservoir Rd.
Dent Pl.
32nd St.
31st St.
Dent Pl.
Avon Ln.
Cambridge Pl.
29th St.
28th St.
Q St.
22nd St.
21st St.
20th St.
Dupont Circle
National Trust
Q St.
O St.
Cloisters
Q St.
Wisconsin Ave.
Volta Pl.
33rd St.
30th St.
P St.
O St.
O St.
Newport Pl.
Sunderland Pl.
Connecticut Ave.
N St.
Jefferson Pl.
Explorers Hall
DeSales St.

36th St.
35th St.
34th St.
P St.
Dumbarton St.
26th St.
27th St.
31st St.
N St.
New Hampshire Ave.
M St.
M St.
19th St.
L St.

37th St.
Prospect St.
Potomac St.
C&O Canal
Grace St.
Thomas Jefferson St.
Olive St.
M St.
Washington Circle
L St.
L St.
K St.

3

Whitehurst Fwy.
South St.
29
Pennsylvania
Ave.
29
66
66
24th St.
23rd St.
22nd St.
H St.
World Bank
Jackson Pl.
Francis Scott Key Br.
Watergate Hotel Complex
George Washington University
G St.
Old Executive Office Bldg.
State Pl.
S. Exec.

N. Moore
Theodore Roosevelt Memorial
Kennedy Center
General Services Bldg.
F St.
E St.
E St.
Virginia Ave.
D St.
17th St.

66
N. Kent
Arlington Ridge
Theodore Roosevelt Island
Dept. of State
C St.
C St.
Ellipse

4
Moyer Dr.
Wilson Blvd.
George Washington Memorial Pkwy.
Theodore Roosevelt Br.
50
66
50
Constitution Ave.

50
Vietnam Veterans Memorial
NW
SW
SE
NE

Iwo Jima Memorial
George Washington
Reflecting Pool
Lincoln Memorial
Korean War Veterans Memorial
Kutz Br.

5
Memorial Dr.
Davis Highway
Jefferson
Arlington Memorial Br.
Memorial Pkwy.
Ladybird Johnson Park
Columbia Island
Independence Ave.
West Potomac Park
Ohio Dr.
Tidal Basin

Memorial Dr.
Holmes
Eisenhower
FDR Memorial
W. Basin Dr.
Potomac River

ARLINGTON NATIONAL CEMETERY
Tomb of the Unknown Soldier

6
VIRGINIA
King
Marshall Dr.
Boundary Dr.
L.B.J. Memorial
395
1
Washington Blvd.
Pentagon

A B C

MAP 5 **Streetfinder/Central Washington DC**

Numbers refer to grid locations on map

Adams Mill Rd. C1
Adams St. E1, F1
Ashmead Pl. C1
Avon La. A2
Avon Pl. A2
Bancroft Pl. B2, C2
Barry Pl. D1, E1
Bates St. E2, F2
Belmont Rd. C1
Belmont St. C1, D1
Benton Pl. B1
Biltmore St. C1
Bryant St. E1, F1
C St. NW, NE B4, F4
C St. SW, SE D5, F5
California St. B1, C1
Calvert St. B1, C1
Cambridge Pl. B2
Canal St. E5, F6
Caroline St. D1
Carrollburg Pl. E6
Champlain St. C1
Channing St. F1, E1
Chapin St. D1
Church St. C2, D2
Cleveland Ave. A1, B2
Clifton St. D1
College St. E1
Columbia Rd. C1, E1
Connecticut Ave. B1, C3
Constitution Ave. B4, F4
Corcoran St. C2, D2
Crescent Pl. C1
Cushing Pl. F6
D St. NW, NE C4, F4
D St. SW, SE D5, F5
Decatur Pl. B2, C2
Delaware Ave. F4
Dent Pl. A2, B2
DeSales St. C3
Duddington Pl. F5
Dumbarton St. A2, B2
Dupont Circle C2
E St. NW, NE B4, F4
E St. SW, SE E5, F5
East Basin Dr. D5
East Capitol St. F4
Eckington Pl. F2
Edgevale Ter. B1
Ellipse Rd. C4, D4
Elm St. E1
Euclid St. C1, D1
F St. NW, NE B4, F4

F St. SW, SE F5
Fairmont St. D1
Flagler Pl. E1
Florida Ave. C2, E1
French St. D2, E2
Fuller St. D1
G St. NW, NE B3, F3
G St. SW, SE D5, F5
George Washington Memorial Pkwy. A3, C6
Georgia Ave. E1
Girard St. D1, F1
Grace St. A3
H St. NW, NE B3, F3
H St. SW, SE E6, F6
Half St. SE F6
Half St. SW E6
Hall Pl. A1
Harvard St. C1, E1
Hawthorne Ave. B1
Henry Bacon Dr. C4
Hobart St. C1
Howard Pl. E1
Howison Pl. E6
I St. NW, NE B3, F3
I St. SW, SE E6, F6
Independence Ave. B5, F5
Indiana Ave. E4
Ivy St. F5
Jackson Pl. C3
Jefferson Dr. D5, E5
Jefferson Pl. C3
Johnson Ave. D2
K St. NW, NE B3, F3
K St. SW, SE E6, F6
Kalorama Circle B1
Kalorama Rd. B1, C1
L St. NW, NE B3, F3
L St. SW, SE E6, F6
Lanier Pl. C1
Lincoln Rd. F1, F2
Logan Circle D2
Louisiana Ave. E4, F4
M St. NW, NE A3, F3
M St. SW, SE E6, F6
Madison Dr. D4, E4
Madison Pl. D3
Maine Ave. D5, E6
Makamie Pl. E6
Market Pl. E4
Maryland Ave. E5, F4
Massachusetts Ave. A1, F3

McGill Ter. B1
McMillan Dr. E1
Memorial Dr. A5, B5
Michigan Ave. E1, F1
Mintwood Pl. C1
Mt. Vernon Sq. E3
N St. NW, NE A3, F2
N St. SW, SE E6, F6
Neal Pl. E2
New Hampshire Ave. B4, D1
New Jersey Ave. E2, F6
New York Ave. C4, F2
Newport Pl. C2
Normanstone Dr. A1, B1
North Capitol St. F1, F4
O St. NW, NE A2, F2
O St. SW, SE E6, F6
Observatory Circle A1
Observatory La. A1
Ohio Dr. C5
Olive St. B3
Ontario Rd. C1
P St. NW, NE A2, F2
Patterson St. F3
Pennsylvania Ave. B3, E4
Pierce St. F3
Potomac St. A2, A3
Prospect St. A3
Q St. A2, F2
Quincy Pl. E2, F2
R St. NW, NE A2, F2
Randolph Pl. E2, F2
Reservoir Rd. A2
Rhode Island Ave. C3, F1
Riggs Pl. C2, D2
Rock Creek & Potomac Pkwy. B1, B4
Rock Creek Dr. B1
S St. NW, NE A2, F2
School St. E5
Scott Circle C2, D2
Seaton Pl. C1, F2
Seaton St. C1
Sheridan Circle B2
Sherman Ave. E1
Shoreham Dr. B1
South St. A3
South Capitol St. F5, F6
South Executive Pl. C4, D4
State Pl. C4

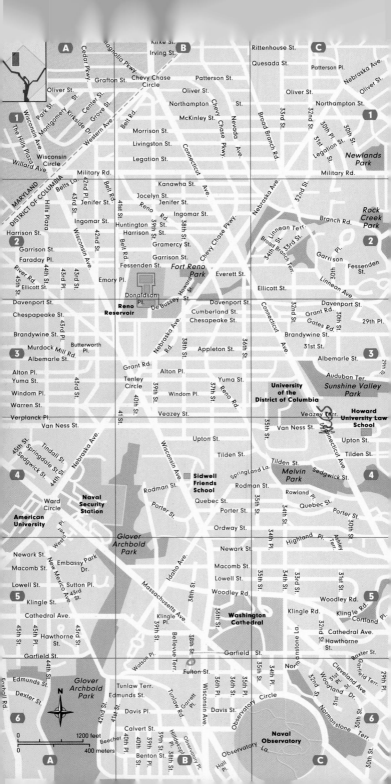

Numbers refer to grid locations on map

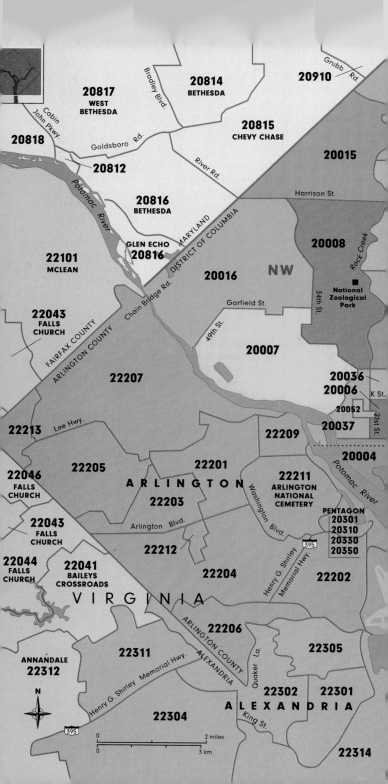

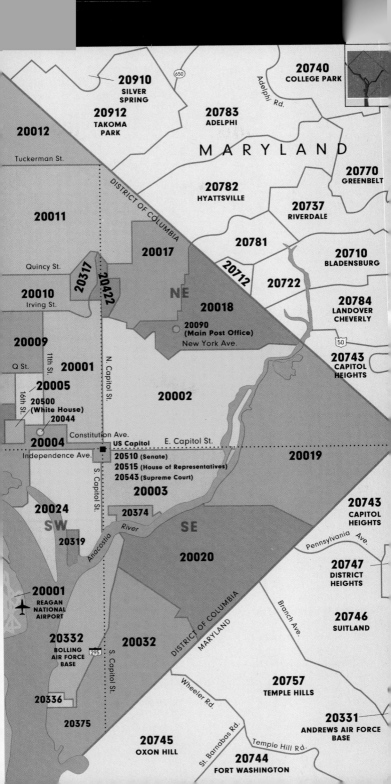

MAP 8

Hospitals & Late-Night Pharmacies

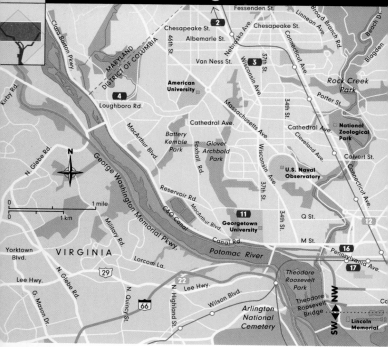

Listed by Site Number

1 Walter Reed Army Medical Center
2 Washington Health Care Group
3 Psychiatric Institute of DC
4 Sibley Memorial
5 Providence

6 Hospital for Sick Children
7 Veterans Affairs Medical Center
8 National Rehabilitation
9 Children's

10 Washington Hospital Center
11 Georgetown University
12 CVS Drug Stores
13 DC General
14 CVS Drug Stores

Listed Alphabetically

HOSPITALS

Capitol Hill, 18.
700 Constitution Ave NE ☎ 675-0500

Children's, 9. 111 Michigan Ave NW
☎ 745-5000

Columbia Hospital for Women, 16.
2425 L St NW ☎ 293-6500

DC General, 13. 1900 Massachusetts
Ave SE ☎ 675-5000

Georgetown University, 11.
3800 Reservoir Rd NW ☎ 687-2000

**George Washington University
Medical Center, 17.** 901 23rd St NW
☎ 994-1000

Greater SE Community, 20.
1310 Southern Ave SE ☎ 574-6000

Hadley Memorial, 21. 4601 Martin
Luther King Jr Ave SW ☎ 574-5700

Hospital for Sick Children, 6.
1731 Bunker Hill Rd NE ☎ 832-4400

Howard University, 15.
2041 Georgia Ave NW ☎ 865-6100

National Rehabilitation, 8.
102 Irving St NW ☎ 877-1000

Providence, 5. 1150 Varnum St NE
☎ 269-7000

Psychiatric Institute of DC, 3.
4228 Wisconsin Ave NW ☎ 965-8200

Sibley Memorial, 4.
5255 Loughboro Rd NW ☎ 537-4000

St Elizabeth's, 19. 2700 Martin Luther
King Jr Ave SE ☎ 562-4000

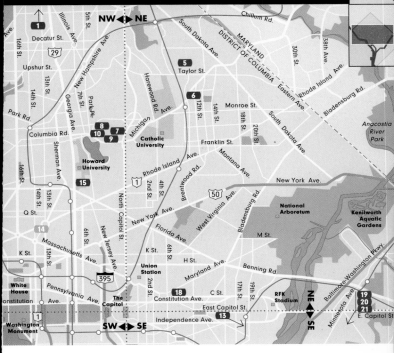

MAP 8

Listed Alphabeticallyr (cont.)

Veterans Affairs Medical Center, 7.
50 Irving St NW ☎ 745-8000

Walter Reed Army Medical Center, 1.
6900 Georgia Ave NW ☎ 782-3501

Washington Hospital Center, 10. 110
Irving St NW ☎ 877-7000

Washington Health Care Group, 2.
5151 Wisconsin Ave NW ☎ 362-1191

LATE-NIGHT/24-HOUR PHARMACIES

CVS Drug Stores, 14.
1211 Vermont Ave NW ☎ 628-0720

CVS Drug Stores, 12.
6-7 Dupont Circle NW ☎ 785-1466

CVS Drug Stores, 22.
3133 Lee Hwy Arlington, VA
☎ 703/522-0260

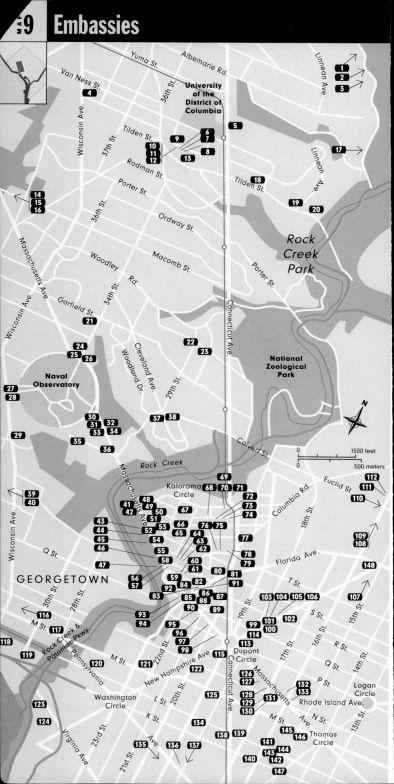

MAP 9 **Embassies**

Afghanistan, 67. 2341 Wyoming Ave NW ☎ 234-3770

Albania, 142. 1511 K St NW ☎ 223-4942

Algeria, 71. 2118 Kalorama Rd NW ☎ 265-2800

Angola, 138. 1050 Connecticut Ave NW ☎ 785-1156

Argentina, 99. 1600 New Hampshire Ave NW ☎ 939-6400

Armenia, 91. 2225 R St NW ☎ 319-1976

Australia, 132. 1601 Massachusetts Ave NW ☎ 797-3000

Austria, 9. 3524 International Ct NW ☎ 895-6700

Azerbaijan, 144. 927 15th St NW ☎ 842-0001

Bahamas, 93. 2220 Massachusetts Ave NW ☎ 319-2660

Bahrain, 11. 3502 International Dr NW ☎ 342-0741

Bangladesh, 28. 2201 Wisconsin Ave NW ☎ 342-8372

Barbados, 73. 2144 Wyoming Ave NW ☎ 939-9200

Belarus, 101. 1619 New Hampshire Ave NW ☎ 986-1604

Belgium, 21. 3330 Garfield St NW ☎ 333-6900

Belize, 41. 2535 Massachusetts Ave NW ☎ 332-9636

Benin, 23. 2737 Cathdral Ave NW ☎ 232-6656

Bolivia, 33. 3014 Massachusetts Ave NW ☎ 483-4410

Bosnia/Herzegovina, 138. 1707 L St NW ☎ 833-3612

Botswana, 10. 3400 Int'l Dr NW ☎ 244-4990

Brazil, 36. 3006 Massachusetts Ave NW ☎ 745-2700

Brunei, 123. 2600 Virginia Ave NW ☎ 342-0159

Bulgaria, 83. 1621 22nd St NW ☎ 387-7969

Burkina Faso, 47. 2340 Massachusetts Ave NW ☎ 332-5577

Burundi, 27. 2233 Wisconsin Ave NW ☎ 342-2574

Cambodia, 109. 4500 16th St NW ☎ 726-7742

Cameroon, 55. 2349 Massachusetts Ave NW ☎ 265-8790

Canada, 135. 501 Pennsylvania Ave NW ☎ 682-1740

Cape Verde, 25. 3415 Massachusetts Ave NW ☎ 965-6820

Central African Republic, 85. 1618 22nd St NW ☎ 483-7800

Chad, 87. 2002 R St NW ☎ 462-4009

Chile, 127. 1732 Massachusetts Ave NW ☎ 785-1746

China (People's Republic), 69. 2300 Connecticut Ave NW ☎ 328-2500

Colombia, 79. 2118 Leroy Pl NW ☎ 387-8338

Congo, 3. 4891 Colorado Ave NW ☎ 726-0825

Costa Rica, 62. 2114 S St NW ☎ 234-2945

Croatia, 52. 2343 Massachusetts Ave NW ☎ 588-5899

Cuban Interests Section, 108. 2630 16th St NW ☎ 797-8518

Cyprus, 61. 2211 R St NW ☎ 462-5772

Czech Republic, 19. 3900 Spring of Freedom St NW ☎ 274-9100

Denmark, 35. 3200 Whitehaven St NW ☎ 234-4300

Djibouti, 145. 1156 15th St NW ☎ 331-0270

Dominican Republic, 82. 1715 22nd St NW ☎ 332-6280

Ecuador, 107. 2535 15th St NW ☎ 234-7200

Egypt, 8. 3522 International Ct NW ☎ 895-5400

El Salvador, 65. 2308 California St NW ☎ 265-9671

Eritrea, 106. 1708 New Hampshire Ave NW ☎ 319-1991

Estonia, 90. 2131 Massachusetts Ave NW ☎ 588-0101

Ethiopia, 70. 2134 Kalorama Rd NW ☎ 234-2281

Fiji, 27. 2233 Wisconsin Ave NW ☎ 337-8320

Finland, 32. 3301 Mass Ave NW ☎ 298-5800

France, 40. 4101 Reservoir Rd NW ☎ 944-6000

Gabon, 89. 2034 20th St NW ☎ 797-1000

Gambia, 144. 1155 15th St NW ☎ 785–1399

Georgia (Republic), 147. 1511 K St NW ☎ 393–5959

Germany, 39. 4645 Reservoir Rd NW ☎ 298–4000

Ghana, 6. 3512 International Dr NW ☎ 686–4520

Great Britain, 31. 3100 Massachusetts Ave NW ☎ 462–1340

Greece, 84. 2221 Massachusetts Ave NW ☎ 939–5800

Grenada, 105. 1701 New Hampshire Ave NW ☎ 265–2561

Guatemala, 59. 2220 R St NW ☎ 745–4952

Guinea, 78. 2112 Leroy Pl NW ☎ 483–9420

Guyana, 50. 2490 Tracy Pl NW ☎ 265–6900

Haiti, 57. 2311 Massachusetts Ave NW ☎ 332–4090

Honduras, 140. 1612 K St NW ☎ 223–0185

Hungary, 20. 3910 Shoemaker St NW ☎ 362–6730

Iceland, 145. 1156 15th St NW ☎ 265–6653

India, 49. 2107 Massachusetts Ave NW ☎ 939–7000

Indonesia, 98. 2020 Massachusetts Ave NW ☎ 775–5200

Iraq, 113. 1801 P St NW ☎ 483–7500

Ireland, 92. 2234 Massachusetts Ave NW ☎ 462–3939

Israel, 7. 3514 International Dr NW ☎ 364–5500

Italy, 110. 1601 Fuller St NW ☎ 328–5500

Ivory Coast, 43. 2424 Massachusetts Ave NW ☎ 483–2400

Jamaica, 114. 1520 New Hampshire Ave NW ☎ 452–0660

Japan, 48. 2520 Massachusetts Ave NW ☎ 939–6700

Jordan, 12. 3504 International Dr NW ☎ 966–2664

Kenya, 60. 2249 R St NW ☎ 387–6101

Korea, 58. 2320 Massachusetts Ave NW ☎ 939–5600

Kuwait, 18. 2940 Tilden St NW ☎ 966–0702

Laos, 63. 2222 S St NW ☎ 332–6416

Latvia, 17. 4325 17th St NW ☎ 726–8213

Lebanon, 38. 2560 28th St NW ☎ 939–6300

Lesotho, 42. 2511 Massachusetts Ave NW ☎ 797–5533

Liberia, 2. 5303 Colorado Ave NW ☎ 723–0437

Lithuania, 111. 2622 16th St NW ☎ 234–5860

Luxembourg, 97. 2200 Massachusetts Ave NW ☎ 265–4171

Madagascar, 46. 2374 Massachusetts Ave NW ☎ 265–5525

Malawi, 44. 2408 Massachusetts Ave NW ☎ 797–1007

Malaysia, 54. 2401 Massachusetts Ave NW ☎ 328–2700

Mali, 86. 2130 R St NW ☎ 332–2249

Malta, 77. 2017 Connecticut Ave NW ☎ 462–3611

Mauritania, 75. 2129 Leroy Pl NW ☎ 232–5700

Mauritius, 5. 4301 Connecticut Ave NW ☎ 244–1491

Mexico, 136. 1911 Pennsylvania Ave NW ☎ 728–1600

Mongolia, 117. 2833 M St NW ☎ 333–7117

Morocco, 88. 1601 21st St NW ☎ 462–7979

Mozambique, 125. 1990 M St NW ☎ 293–7146

Myanmar, 64. 2300 S St NW ☎ 332–9044

Namibia, 103. 1605 New Hampshire Ave NW ☎ 986–0540

Nepal, 76. 2131 Leroy Pl NW ☎ 667–4550

Netherlands, 4. 4200 Linnean Ave NW ☎ 244–5300

New Zealand, 30. 37 Observatory Circle NW ☎ 328–4800

Nicaragua, 104. 1627 New Hampshire Ave NW ☎ 939–6570

Niger, 80. 2204 R St NW ☎ 483–4224

Nigeria, 115. 2201 M St NW ☎ 822–1500

Norway, 24. 2720 34th St NW ☎ 333–6000

MAP 9

Listed Alphabetically (cont.)

Oman, 68. 2535 Belmont Rd NW
☎ 387-1980

Pakistan, 56. 2315 Massachusetts
Ave NW ☎ 939-6200

Panama, 37. 2862 McGill Ter NW
☎ 483-1407

Paraguay, 45. 2400 Massachusetts
Ave NW ☎ 483-6960

Peru, 130. 1700 Massachusetts Ave
NW ☎ 833-9860

Philippines, 131. 1600 Massachusetts
Ave NW ☎ 467-9300

Poland, 112. 2640 16th St NW
☎ 234-3800

Portugal, 66. 2310 Tracy Pl NW
☎ 332-3007

Qatar, 4. 4200 Wisconsin Ave NW
☎ 274-1600

Romania, 94. 1607 23rd St NW
☎ 232-4747

Russia, 141. 1125 16th St NW
☎ 232-6020

Rwanda, 102. 1714 New Hampshire
Ave NW ☎ 232-2882

San Marino, 134. 1899 L St NW
☎ 223-3517

Saudi Arabia, 124. 601 New
Hampshire Ave NW ☎ 342-3800

Senegal, 74. 2112 Wyoming Ave NW
☎ 234-0540

Singapore, 13. 3501 International Pl
NW ☎ 537-3100

Slovakia, 28. 2201 Wisconsin Ave NW
☎ 965-5160

Slovenia, 148. 1525 New Hampshire
Ave NW ☎ 667-5363

South Africa, 34. 3051 Massachusetts
Ave NW ☎ 232-4400

Spain, 120. 2375 Pennsylvania Ave
NW ☎ 452-0100

Sri Lanka, 72. 2148 Wyoming Ave NW
☎ 483-4025

St. Kitts and Nevis, 14. 3216 New
Mexico Ave NW ☎ 686-2636

St Lucia, 15. 3216 New Mexico Ave
NW ☎ 364-6792

St. Vincent and The Grenadines, 16.
3216 New Mexico Ave NW
☎ 364-6730

Sudan, 95. 2210 Massachusetts Ave
NW ☎ 338-8565

Surinam, 5. 4301 Connecticut Ave NW
☎ 244-7488

Swaziland, 10. 3007 Tilden St
NW ☎ 362-6683

Sweden, 145. 1501 M St NW
☎ 467-2600

Switzerland, 21. 2900 Cathedral Ave
NW ☎ 745-7900

Syria, 68. 2215 Wyoming Ave NW
☎ 232-6313

Tanzania, 81. 2139 R St NW
☎ 939-6125

Thailand, 29. 1024 Wisconsin Ave NW
☎ 944-3600

Togo, 95.
2208 Massachusetts Ave NW
☎ 234-4212

Trinidad & Tobago, 129. 1708
Massachusetts Ave NW ☎ 467-6490

Tunisia, 133. 1515 Massachusetts Ave
NW ☎ 862-1850

Turkey, 128. 1714 Massachusetts Ave
NW ☎ 387-3200

Uganda, 1.
5909 16th St NW ☎ 726-7100

Ukraine, 116. 3350 M St NW
☎ 333-0606

United Arab Emirates, 118.
3000 K St NW ☎ 338-6500

Uruguay, 137. 1918 F St NW
☎ 331-1313

Uzbekistan, 124. 1746 Massachusetts
Ave NW ☎ 887-5300

Vatican, 26. 3339 Massachusetts Ave
NW ☎ 333-7121

Venezuela, 119. 1099 30th St NW
☎ 342-2214

Vietnam, 122. 1233 20th St NW
☎ 861-0737

Yugoslavia, 53. 2410 California St
NW ☎ 462-6566

Zambia, 51. 2419 Massachusetts Ave
NW ☎ 265-9717

Zimbabwe, 100. 1608 New
Hampshire Ave NW ☎ 332-7100

MAP
10

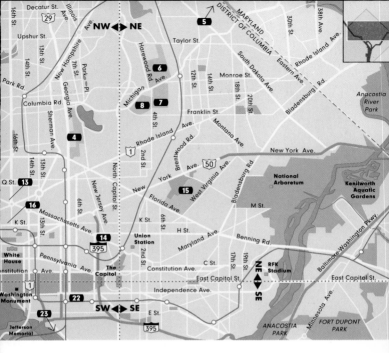

Listed by Site Number

1 National Library of Medicine
2 National Agricultural
3 Cleveland Park
4 Petworth
5 Mt Pleasant
6 Georgetown Regional
7 Dumbarton Oaks
8 Alexander Graham Bell Association
9 Sumner School Archives
10 West End
11 Foundation Center
12 Federal Bar Foundation
13 Performing Arts
14 National Academy of Sciences
15 Organization of American States

Listed Alphabetically

Air & Space, 24. Independence Ave & 6th St SW ☎ 357-3133

Alexander Graham Bell Assn, 8. 3417 Volta Pl NW ☎ 337-5220

American Art/Portrait Gallery, 18. G & 8th Sts NW ☎ 357-1886

American History, 21. Constitution Ave & 14th St SW ☎ 357-2414

Anacostia Branch, 30. Good Hope Rd & 18th St SE ☎ 729-1329

Arts & Industries, 23. 900 Jefferson Dr SW ☎ 786-2271

Cleveland Park, 3. 3310 Connecticut Ave NW ☎ 727-1345

Daughters of the American Revolution, 16. 1776 D St NW ☎ 628-1776

Dumbarton Oaks, 7. 1703 32nd St NW ☎ 339-6980

Federal Bar Foundation, 12. 1815 H St NW ☎ 638-1956

Folger Shakespeare, 28. 201 E Capitol St SE ☎ 544-4600

Foundation Center, 11. 1001 Connecticut Ave NW ☎ 331-1400

Georgetown Regional, 6. 3260 R St NW ☎ 727-1353

Library of Congress, 27. 10 Independence Ave SE ☎ 707-5000

Martin Luther King Jr Memorial, 17. 901 G St NW ☎ 727-1111

Mt Pleasant, 5. Lamont St & 16th St NW ☎ 727-1361

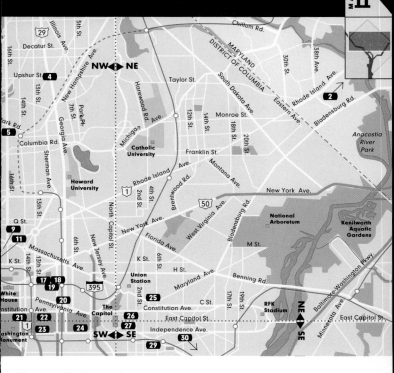

Listed by Site Number (cont.)

Listed Alphabetically

MAP 12 Airports

Terminal C
Terminal B

North Concourse

27 26   24 23 22 21

Terminal A

20
19
18B
18A

15   16   17
11 12 14

Lot D
(short term)

Thomas Ave.

Lot A
(short term)

9   10

8A

Smith Blvd.

Lot B
(hourly/daily parking)

Lot C
(short term)

8   7   6
5

Lot C
(hourly/daily parking)

M

NATIONAL AIRPORT

1A

1 2 3

Budget

Parking Garage
(Hertz Upper Level)

Avis

National

National

E. Abingdon Dr.

← TO WASHINGTON, RT. 395

George Washington Memorial Pkwy.

Thomas Ave. (lower level)

Smith Blvd. (upper level)

South Hangers

N

Reagan National Airport

TO RT.1, RT.495, ALEXANDRIA

TO SATELLITE LOTS A & B

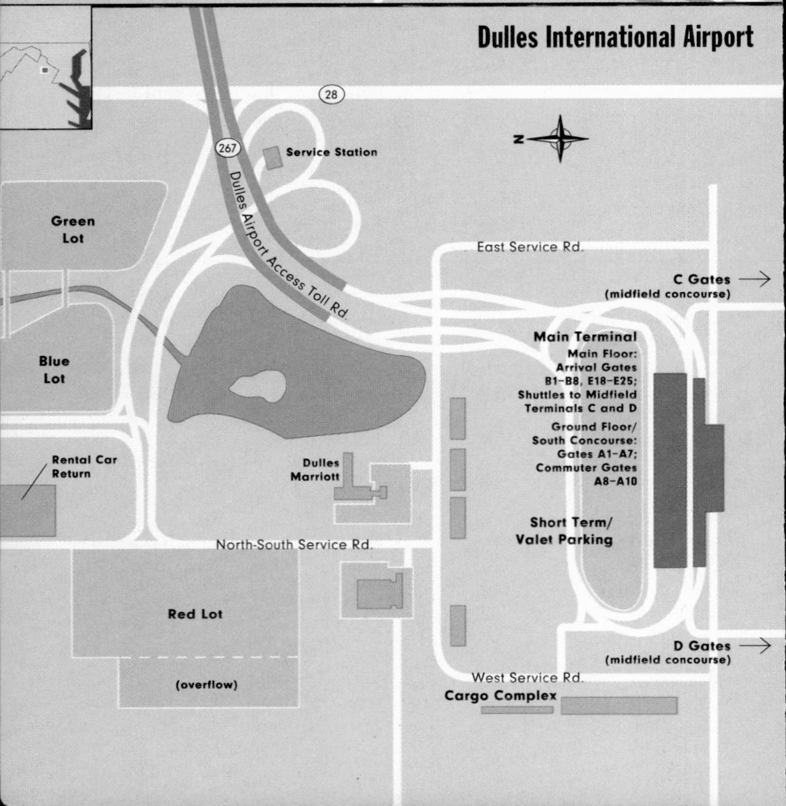

Dulles International Airport

28

267

Service Station

Dulles Airport Access Toll Rd.

N

Green Lot

East Service Rd.

C Gates
(midfield concourse) →

Blue Lot

Main Terminal
Main Floor:
Arrival Gates
B1–B8, E18–E25;
Shuttles to Midfield
Terminals C and D

Ground Floor/
South Concourse:
Gates A1–A7;
Commuter Gates
A8–A10

Rental Car Return

Dulles Marriott

Short Term/ Valet Parking

North-South Service Rd.

Red Lot

(overflow)

West Service Rd.

D Gates
(midfield concourse) →

Cargo Complex

Baltimore-Washington International Airport

Airline Terminals

AIRLINES	REAGAN/NAT'L	DULLES	BWI
Aeroflot ☎ 800/955–5555		B	
Air Canada ☎ 800/776–3000	B	C	
Air France ☎ 800/321–4538		B	
Air Jamaica ☎ 800/523–5585			E
Air Tran ☎ 800/247–8726		D	
All Nippon (ANA) ☎ 800/235–9262		B	
America West ☎ 800/235–9292	B	B	C
American ☎ 800/433–7300	B	D	C
American Eagle ☎ 800/433–7300	B		
British Airways ☎ 800/247–9297		D	E
Continental ☎ 800/525–0280	B	B	C
Continental Express ☎ 800/525–0280	B	B	
Delta ☎ 800/221–1212	B	B	B
DeltaConnection ☎ 800/221–1212	B	B	
Delta Shuttle ☎ 800/221–1212	B		
El Al Israel ☎ 800/352–5747			E
Icelandair ☎ 800/223–5500			E
KLM ☎ 800/374–7747		B	
Lufthansa ☎ 800/645–3880		C	
Mexican ☎ 800/531–7921			E
Midway ☎ 800/446–4392	A		C
Midwest Express ☎ 800/452–2022		A	
Northwest ☎ 800/225–2525	A	B	C
Saudi Arabian ☎ 800/472–8342		A	
Southwest ☎ 800/435–9792			C
Spanair ☎ 888/545–5757		A	
TWA ☎ 800/221–2000	A	D	D
United ☎ 800/241–6522	B	C,D	A,B
United Express ☎ 800/241–6522		A	
US Airways ☎ 800/428–4322	B,C	B	D
US Airways Express ☎ 800/428–4322	C		
US Airways Shuttle ☎ 800/428–4322	C		
Virgin Atlantic ☎ 800/468–8621		B	

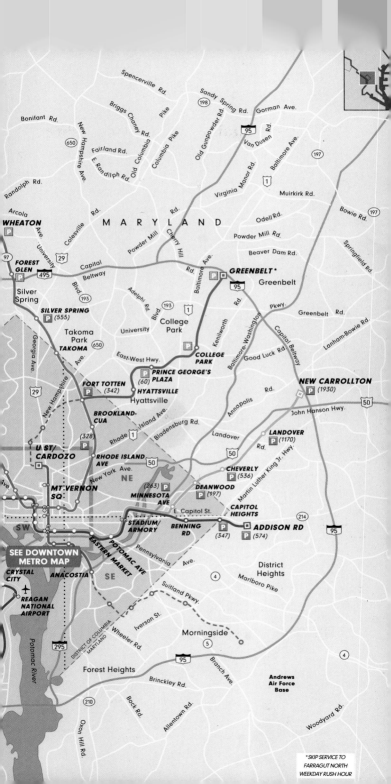

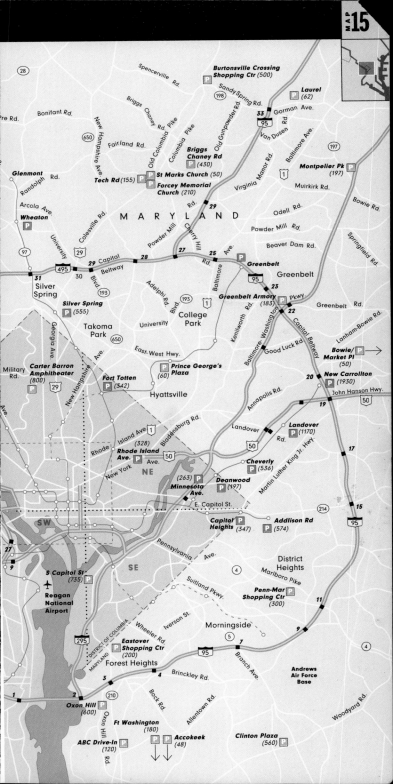

MAP **15**

28

Spencerville Rd.

Burtonsville Crossing Shopping Ctr (500) P

Laurel (62) P

198 Sandy Spring Rd.

Bonifant Rd.

Pre Rd.

Briggs Chaney Rd. Pike

33 Gorman Ave.

95

Van Dusen Rd.

Baltimore Ave.

197

650 Fairland Rd.

Columbia Pike

Old Columbia Pike

Old Gunpowder Rd.

New Hampshire Ave.

Randolph Rd.

Glenmont ○

Briggs Chaney Rd (430) P

St Marks Church (50) P

Tech Rd (155) P

Forcey Memorial Church (210) P

Virginia Manor Rd.

1

Montpelier Pk (197) P

Muirkirk Rd.

Bowie Rd.

Arcola Ave.

Wheaton ○ P

Coleville Rd.

M A R Y L A N D

Rd.

29

Odell Rd.

Powder Mill Rd.

Beaver Dam Rd.

Springfield Rd.

97 University

650

29 Capital

Powder Mill Rd.

27 Rd.

Cherry Hill Rd.

25 Ave.

Greenbelt P

31 495 30 Beltway

28

Baltimore Ave.

95

Greenbelt

Silver Spring

193

Adelphi Rd.

193 Blvd.

1

Greenbelt Armory (183) P

23

Greenbelt Pkwy.

Greenbelt Rd.

Silver Spring (555) P

Takoma Park

University

College Park

Kenilworth Rd.

Baltimore-Washington Pkwy.

Capital Beltway

22

Lanham-Bowie Rd.

Georgia Ave.

650

East-West Hwy.

Good Luck Rd.

Bowie/ Market Pl (50) →

Military Rd.

Carter Barron Amphitheater (800) P 29

New Hampshire Ave.

Fort Totten (342) P

Prince George's Plaza (60) P

Hyattsville

Annapolis Rd.

20 **New Carrollton (1930)** P

John Hanson Hwy.

50

19

Ave.

Rhode Island Ave 1 (328)

Bladensburg Rd.

Landover Rd.

Landover (1170) P

17

Rhode Island Ave. (263) P

New York

Rhode Island

50

NE

Cheverly (536) P

Martin Luther King Jr. Hwy.

Deanwood (197) P

Minnesota Ave. (263) P

E. Capitol St.

214

15

95

SW

Capitol Heights (347) P

Addison Rd (574) P

27

9

Pennsylvania

SE

Ave.

District Heights

Marlboro Pike

11

S Capitol St (735) P

Suitland Pkwy.

4

Penn-Mar Shopping Ctr (300) P

Reagan National Airport ✈

Wheeler Rd.

Iverson St.

Morningside

9

295

Eastover Shopping Ctr (200) P

5

7

Branch Ave.

Andrews Air Force Base

Forest Heights

DISTRICT OF COLUMBIA

MARYLAND

Brinckley Rd.

95

3

4

1

2

Oxon Hill (600) P

210

Bock Rd.

Allentown Rd.

Oxon Hill

Rd.

4

Woodyard Rd.

Ft Washington (180) P

Accokeek (48) P

Clinton Plaza (560) P

ABC Drive-In (120)

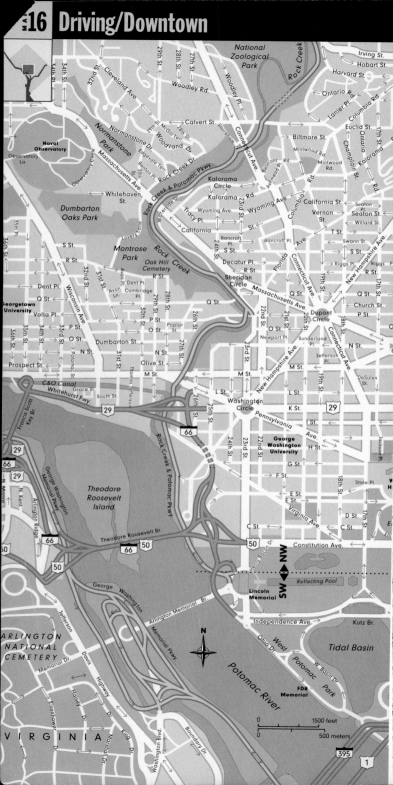

MAP **16**

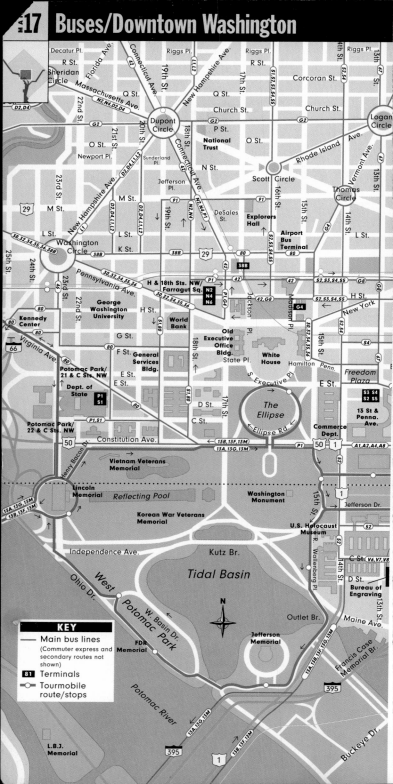

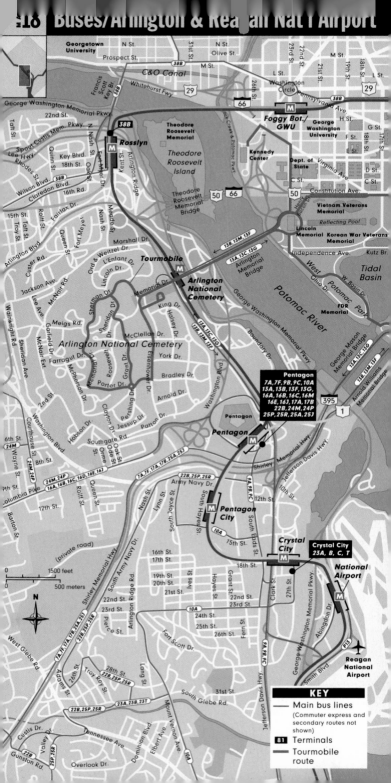

Georgetown University
N St.
Olive St.
N St.
M St.
Prospect St.
C&O Canal
38B
M St.
Whitehurst Fwy
29
Washington Circle
Pennsylvania Ave
38B
29
George Washington Memorial Pkwy
66
Foggy Bot./GWU
George Washington University
H St.
G St.
F St.
22nd St.
Francis Scott Key Br.
38B
Theodore Roosevelt Memorial
Kennedy Center
Dept. of State
Virginia Ave.
E St.
D St.
C St.
38B
Rosslyn
Theodore Roosevelt Island
50
66
Constitution Ave.
50
Theodore Roosevelt Memorial Bridge
Vietnam Veterans Memorial
Reflecting Pool
Lincoln Memorial
Korean War Veterans Memorial
Independence Ave.
Kutz Br.
Tidal Basin
15B, 15M, 15F
Tourmobile
Arlington National Cemetery
13A, 13C, 13G
Arlington Memorial Bridge
Potomac River
FDR Memorial
Arlington National Cemetery
13A, 13C, 13G
18M, 13M, 13F
13B, 13M, 13F
13A, 13C, 13G
George Mason Memorial Bridge
Arnold Williams Memorial Bridge
395
1

Pentagon
7A, 7F, 9B, 9C, 10A
13A, 13B, 13F, 13G,
16A, 16B, 16C, 16M
16E, 16J, 17A, 17B
22B, 24M, 24P
25P, 25R, 25A, 25J

Pentagon
Pentagon
Shirley Memorial Hwy.
Jefferson Davis Hwy.
24M
7A, 7F, 17A, 17B, 25A, 25J
9A, 9B, 9C
24M, 24P
22B, 25P, 25R
24M, 24P
Army Navy Dr.
16A, 16B, 16C, 16D, 16E, 16J
Pentagon City
9A, 9B, 9C
Columbia Pike
10A
Crystal City
Crystal City
23A, B, C, T
National Airport
10A
Reagan National Airport
7A, 7F, 17A, 17B, 25A, 25J
22B, 25P, 25R
23A, 25B, 25J
22B, 25P, 25R
22B
25P, 25R

0   1500 feet
0   500 meters
N

Kirke St.

Irving St.

Rittenhouse St.

Hesketh St.

Magnolia Pkwy.

Grafton St.

Quesada St.

Oliver St.

Cedar Pkwy.

Park St.

Kirkside Dr.

Grove St.

Patterson St.

32nd St.

30th Pl. St.

Oliver St.

Oliver St.

Chevy Chase Circle
L1,L2

Northampton St.

30th St.

McKinley St.

Morrison St.

E6, E7

E2, E4, E6

Chevy Chase Pkwy.

Nevada Ave.

Broad Branch Rd.

33rd St.

Newlands Park

Friendship Heights
E2,E4,E6,L8,
N2,N6,N8,
T2,T6,
30,32,34,36

Livingston St.

Legation St.

Military Rd.

51st St.

Legation St.

M4

Military Rd.

E2, E4

Kanawha St.

Connecticut Ave.

32nd St.

Belts La.

42nd Pl.

Friendship Heights

M

Jocelyn St.

Jenifer St.

Reno Rd.

Nebraska Ave.

Western Ave.

N2, N4

Belts Rd.

43rd St.

Jenifer St.

Ingomar St.

38th St.

Branch Rd.

Hills Plaza

Reno Rd.

39th St.

Ingomar St.

Huntington St.

Linnean Terr.

Harrison St.

42nd St.

41st St.

Belt Rd.

Harrison St.

Gramercy St.

Chevy Chase Pkwy.

Broad Branch Terr.

33rd St.

34th St.

Garrison St.

Garrison St.

Faraday Pl.

Wisconsin Ave.

43rd St.

Garrison St.

Linnean Ave.

Fessenden St.

River Rd.

44th St.

Fessenden St.

Fort Reno Park

Everett St.

32nd St.

45th St.

Ellicott St.

43rd St.

Emory Pl.

DeBussey St.

Davenport St.

Ellicott St.

Grant Rd.

30th St.

Davenport St.

Davenport St.

Donaldson Pl.

Cumberland St.

Gates Rd.

29th Pl.

Chesapeake St.

Howard

Nebraska Ave.

Chesapeake St.

Connecticut

36th St.

Brandywine St.

Brandywine St.

Brandywine St.

Brandywine St.

31st St.

Murdock Mill

Butterworth Pl.

Appleton St.

Albemarle St.

Albemarle St.

Alton Pl.

Rd.

29th St.

GSNC

Audubon Ter.

Tenleytown M Grant

Tenleytown 37

Alton Pl.

Sunshine Valley Park

Yuma St.

H2, H4

Tenley Circle

39th St.

Windom Pl.

Yuma St.

University of the District of Columbia

Van Ness/ UDC

Windom Pl.

38th Pl.

37th St.

Reno Rd.

M

Warren St.

Is shap.

VanNess/UDC

Howard University Law School

Verplanck Pl.

St.

Veazey St.

Van Ness St.

35th St.

Upton St.

Van Ness St.

Upton St.

45th St.

Nebraska Ave.

Tindall St.

Wisconsin Ave.

Tilden St.

H2

Tilden St.

L1, L2

N2, N4

Springdale St.

30,31,33,35,36,H2

Sedgwick St.

Melvin Park

Connecticut Ave.

Sedgwick St.

Springland La.

Sidwell Friends School

Rodman St.

Rowland Pl.

American University

Rodman St.

35th St.

Quebec St.

34th St.

Quebec St.

Porter St.

Wesley Heights
N3

Naval Security Station

Porter St.

H4

Porter St.

30th St.

M

Newark St.

New Mexico Ave.

West

Ordway St.

Highland Pl.

Cleveland Park

Glover Archbold Park

Idaho Ave.

McLean Gardens 96

Newark St.

Ashby Terr.

N4

Macomb St.

Embassy Park Dr.

Macomb St.

35th St.

33rd St.

31st St.

Lowell St.

Sutton Pl.

Massachusetts Ave.

Lowell St.

34th St.

Woodley Rd.

Klingle St.

N2

Woodley Rd.

Klingle Rd.

Klingle Rd.

32nd St.

Cortland

Cathedral Ave.

38th St.

36th St.

Cathedral Ave.

45th Pl.

43rd St.

Hawthorne St.

Klingle Pl.

Washington Cathedral

Hawthorne St.

Baxter St.

Garfield St.

Bellevue Terr.

Garfield St.

35th St.

Woodland Ave.

Gates Rd.

Edmunds St.

Watson St.

39th St.

Fulton St.

36th Pl.

34th St.

Cleveland Ave.

Dexter St.

Glover Archbold Park

42nd St.

Tunlaw Terr.

Edmunds St.

Tunlaw Rd.

Garfield Pl.

36th St.

35th Pl.

Normanstone

31st St.

Woodland Ter.

Foothall Rd.

N

Glover Park D2

41st St.

Davis Pl.

39th St.

Davis St.

Observatory

Wisconsin Ave.

35th St.

36th Pl.

Calvert St.

Beecher St.

40th Pl.

40th St.

Benton St.

D2

30,32,34,36

Naval Observatory

Circle

N2, N4

0   1200 feet

0   400 meters

Cab Zones

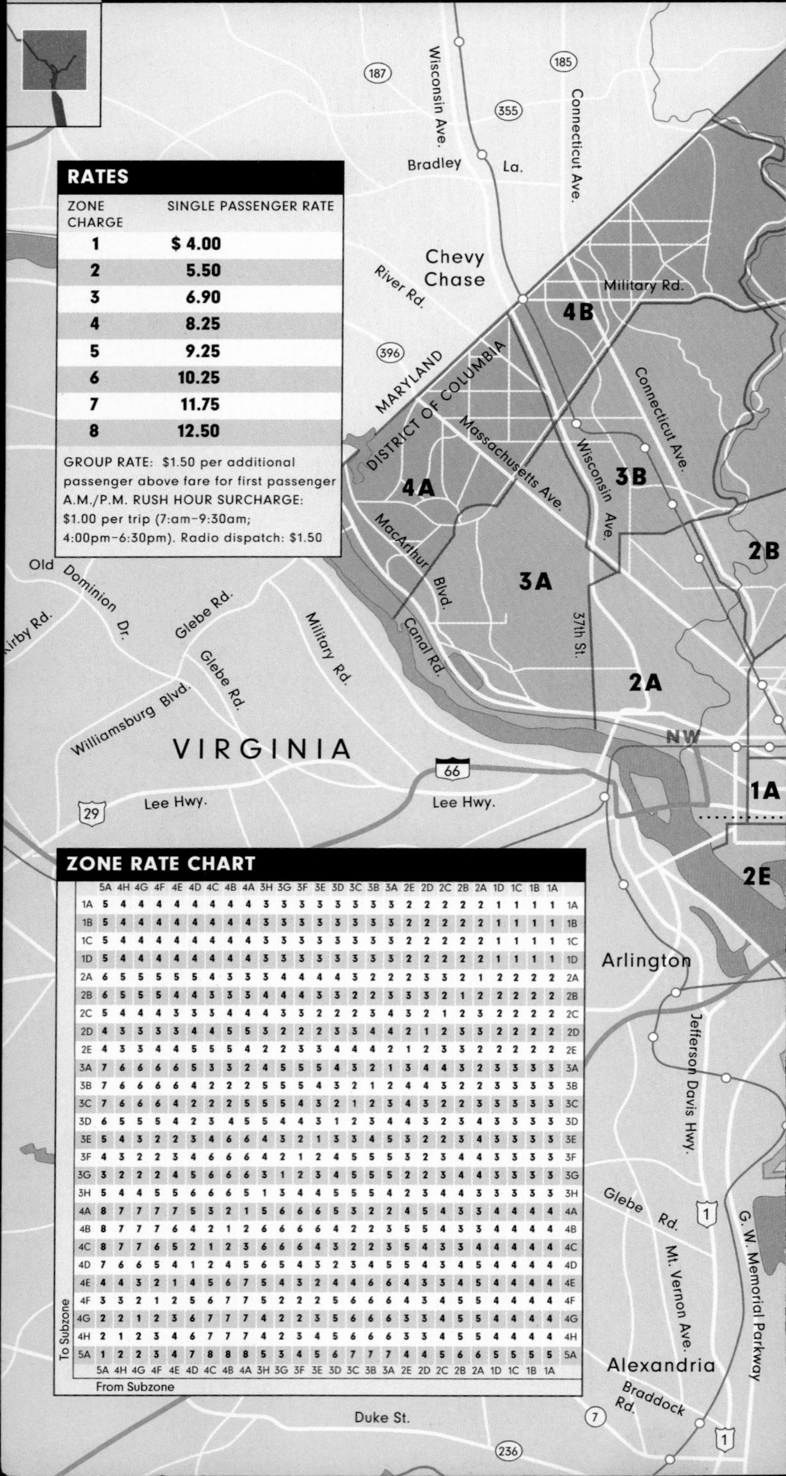
Wisconsin Ave.
187
185
355
Connecticut Ave.
Bradley
La.
Chevy Chase
River Rd.
Military Rd.
4B
396
MARYLAND
DISTRICT OF COLUMBIA
Massachusetts Ave.
Connecticut Ave.
Wisconsin Ave.
3B
4A
MacArthur Blvd.
3A
2B
37th St.
Canal Rd.
2A
Old Dominion Dr.
Kirby Rd.
Glebe Rd.
Military Rd.
Glebe Rd.
Williamsburg Blvd.
VIRGINIA
NW
66
1A
29
Lee Hwy.
Lee Hwy.
2E
Arlington
Jefferson Davis Hwy.
Glebe Rd.
1
G. W. Memorial Parkway
Mt. Vernon Ave.
Alexandria
Braddock Rd.
7
Duke St.
1
236

RATES

ZONE CHARGE	SINGLE PASSENGER RATE
1	$ 4.00
2	5.50
3	6.90
4	8.25
5	9.25
6	10.25
7	11.75
8	12.50

GROUP RATE: $1.50 per additional passenger above fare for first passenger A.M./P.M. RUSH HOUR SURCHARGE: $1.00 per trip (7:am–9:30am; 4:00pm–6:30pm). Radio dispatch: $1.50

ZONE RATE CHART

To Subzone

	5A	4H	4G	4F	4E	4D	4C	4B	4A	3H	3G	3F	3E	3D	3C	3B	3A	2E	2D	2C	2B	2A	1D	1C	1B	1A	
1A	5	4	4	4	4	4	4	4	4	3	3	3	3	3	3	3	3	2	2	2	2	2	1	1	1	1	1A
1B	5	4	4	4	4	4	4	4	4	3	3	3	3	3	3	3	3	2	2	2	2	2	1	1	1	1	1B
1C	5	4	4	4	4	4	4	4	4	3	3	3	3	3	3	3	3	2	2	2	2	2	1	1	1	1	1C
1D	5	4	4	4	4	4	4	4	4	3	3	3	3	3	3	3	3	2	2	2	2	2	1	1	1	1	1D
2A	6	5	5	5	5	5	4	3	3	3	4	4	4	4	3	2	2	2	3	3	2	1	2	2	2	2	2A
2B	6	5	5	5	4	4	3	3	3	4	4	4	3	3	2	2	3	3	3	2	1	2	2	2	2	2	2B
2C	5	4	4	4	3	3	3	4	4	4	3	3	2	2	2	3	4	3	2	1	2	3	2	2	2	2	2C
2D	4	3	3	3	3	4	4	5	5	3	2	2	2	3	3	4	4	2	1	2	3	3	2	2	2	2	2D
2E	4	3	3	4	4	5	5	5	4	2	2	3	3	4	4	4	2	1	2	3	3	2	2	2	2	2	2E
3A	7	6	6	6	6	5	3	3	2	4	5	5	5	4	3	2	1	3	4	4	3	2	3	3	3	3	3A
3B	7	6	6	6	6	4	2	2	2	5	5	5	4	3	2	1	2	4	4	3	2	2	3	3	3	3	3B
3C	7	6	6	6	4	2	2	2	5	5	5	4	3	2	1	2	3	4	3	2	2	3	3	3	3	3	3C
3D	6	5	5	5	4	2	3	4	5	5	4	4	3	1	2	3	4	4	3	2	3	4	3	3	3	3	3D
3E	5	4	3	2	2	3	4	6	6	4	3	2	1	3	3	4	5	3	2	2	3	4	3	3	3	3	3E
3F	4	3	2	2	3	4	6	6	6	4	2	1	2	4	5	5	5	3	2	3	4	4	3	3	3	3	3F
3G	3	2	2	2	4	5	6	6	6	3	1	2	3	4	5	5	5	2	2	3	4	4	3	3	3	3	3G
3H	5	4	4	5	5	6	6	6	5	1	3	4	4	5	5	5	4	2	3	4	4	3	3	3	3	3	3H
4A	8	7	7	7	7	5	3	2	1	5	6	6	6	5	3	2	2	4	5	4	3	3	4	4	4	4	4A
4B	8	7	7	7	6	4	2	1	2	6	6	6	6	4	2	2	3	5	5	4	3	3	4	4	4	4	4B
4C	8	7	7	6	5	2	1	2	3	6	6	6	4	3	2	2	3	5	4	3	3	4	4	4	4	4	4C
4D	7	6	6	5	4	1	2	4	5	6	5	4	3	2	3	4	5	5	4	3	4	5	4	4	4	4	4D
4E	4	4	3	2	1	4	5	6	7	5	4	3	2	4	4	6	6	4	3	3	4	5	4	4	4	4	4E
4F	3	3	2	1	2	5	6	7	7	5	2	2	2	5	6	6	6	4	3	4	5	5	4	4	4	4	4F
4G	2	2	1	2	3	6	7	7	7	4	2	2	3	5	6	6	6	3	3	4	5	5	4	4	4	4	4G
4H	2	1	2	3	4	6	7	7	7	4	2	3	4	5	6	6	6	3	3	4	5	5	4	4	4	4	4H
5A	1	2	2	3	4	7	8	8	8	5	3	4	5	6	7	7	7	4	4	5	6	6	5	5	5	5	5A
	5A	4H	4G	4F	4E	4D	4C	4B	4A	3H	3G	3F	3E	3D	3C	3B	3A	2E	2D	2C	2B	2A	1D	1C	1B	1A	

From Subzone

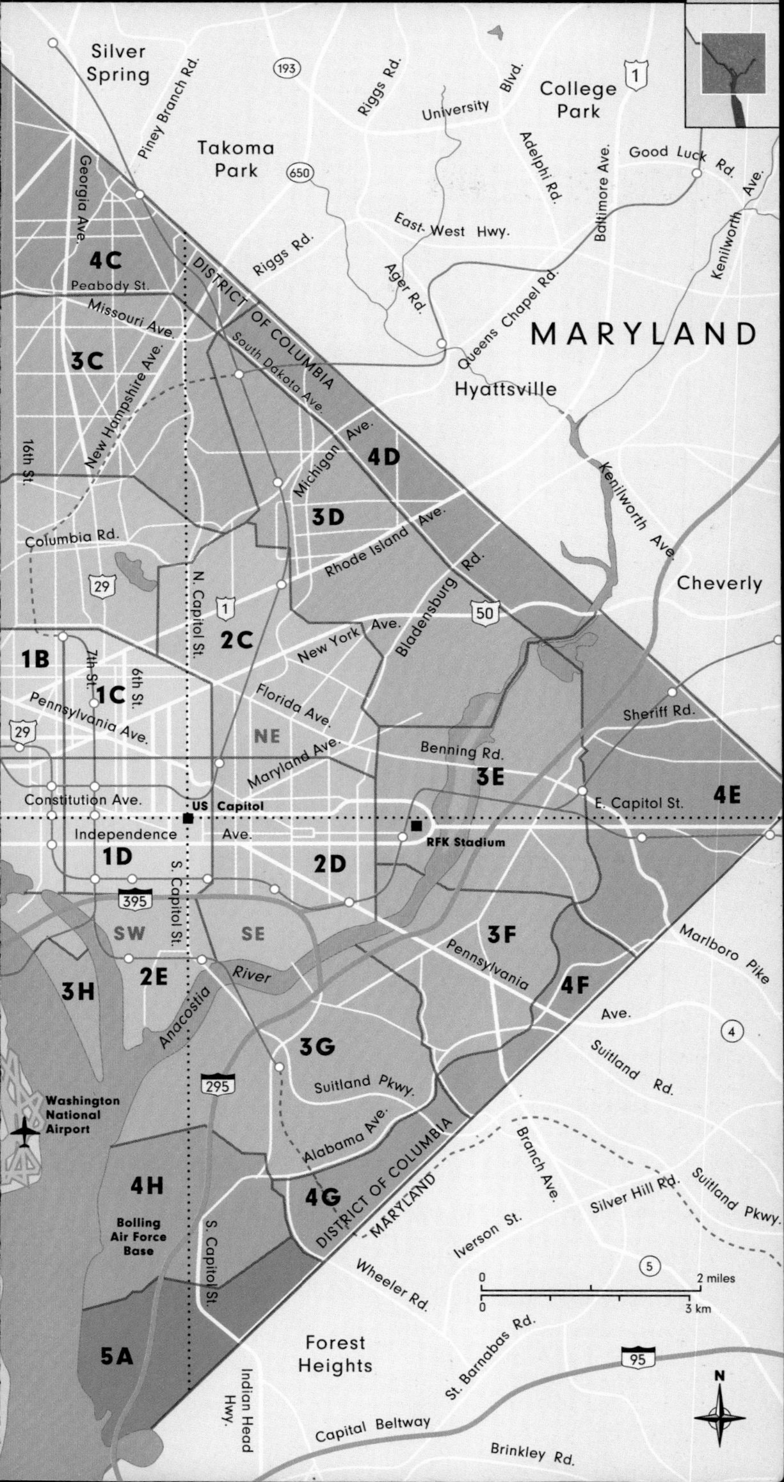

MAP 20

Silver Spring

193

University Blvd.

College Park

1

Good Luck Rd.

Piney Branch Rd.

Takoma Park

650

Riggs Rd.

Adelphi Rd.

Baltimore Ave.

Kenilworth Ave.

Georgia Ave.

DISTRICT OF COLUMBIA

East-West Hwy.

4C

Peabody St.

Missouri Ave.

New Hampshire Ave.

3C

South Dakota Ave.

Riggs Rd.

Ager Rd.

Queens Chapel Rd.

M A R Y L A N D

Hyattsville

Kenilworth Ave.

Cheverly

16th St.

Columbia Rd.

29

N. Capitol St.

1

Michigan Ave.

4D

3D

Rhode Island Ave.

Bladensburg Rd.

50

1B

7th St.

6th St.

1C

Pennsylvania Ave.

2C

New York Ave.

Florida Ave.

29

NE

Maryland Ave.

Benning Rd.

Sheriff Rd.

3E

4E

Constitution Ave.

US Capitol

E. Capitol St.

Independence

Ave.

RFK Stadium

1D

S. Capitol St.

2D

395

SW

SE

3F

Pennsylvania

Marlboro Pike

2E

River

4F

4

3H

Anacostia

3G

Suitland Pkwy.

Suitland Rd.

Washington National Airport

295

Alabama Ave.

DISTRICT OF COLUMBIA

Silver Hill Rd.

Suitland Pkwy.

4H

Bolling Air Force Base

S. Capitol St.

4G

MARYLAND

Branch Ave.

Iverson St.

5

2 miles

3 km

5A

Forest Heights

Indian Head Hwy.

Wheeler Rd.

St. Barnabas Rd.

95

Capital Beltway

Brinkley Rd.

N

MAP 21 **Top Attractions**

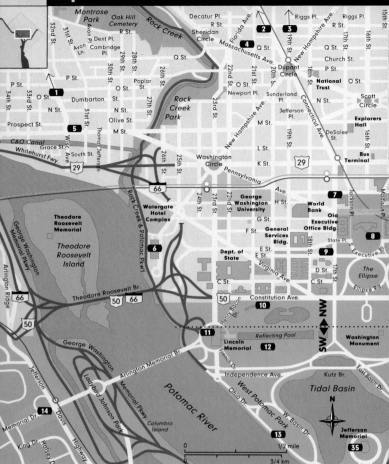

MAP **21**

MAP 22 Exploring the Mall and Vicinity

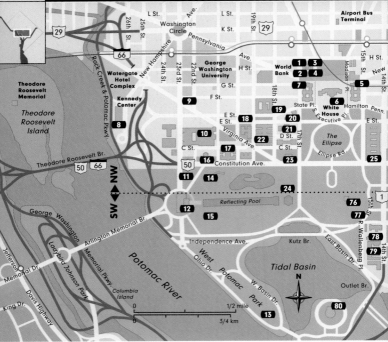

Listed by Site Number

MAP 22

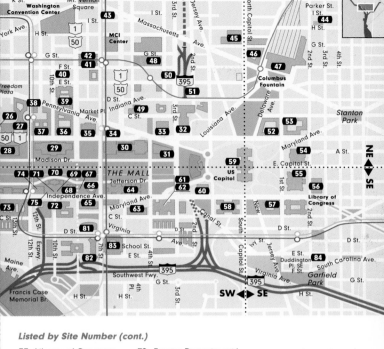

MAP 22 — Exploring the Mall and Vicinity

Listed Alphabetically

Alcohol, Tobacco & Firearms, 43. 650 Massachusetts Ave NW ☎ 927-7777

Arts and Industries Bldg, 68. 900 Jefferson Dr SW ☎ 357-2700

Blair House, 4. 1651 Pennsylvania Ave NW ☎ 879-7880

Bureau of Engraving & Printing, 79. 1400 C St SW ☎ 874-3019

Cannon House Office Building, 57. 25 Independence Ave SE ☎ 224-3121

Capital Children's Museum, 44. 800 3rd St NE ☎ 675-4120

Civil Service, 18. 1900 E St NW ☎ 606-0500

Constitution Gardens, 24. Between Washington Monument & Lincoln Memorial

Corcoran Gallery, 20. New York Ave & 17th St NW ☎ 639-1700

Customs Service, 26. 1301 Constitution Ave NW ☎ 927-6724

DAR Museum, 21. 1776 D St NW ☎ 879-3254

DC Superior Court, 49. 500 Indiana Ave NW ☎ 879-1010

Decatur House, 3. 748 Jackson Pl NW ☎ 842-0920

Department of Agriculture, 73. 1200 Independence Ave SW ☎ 720-2791

Department of Commerce, 25. Constitution Ave & 14th St NW ☎ 482-2000

Department of Education, 63. 600 Independence Ave SW ☎ 401-2000

Dept of Energy/Forrestal Building, 72. 1000 Independence Ave SW ☎ 586-5000

Department of Health & Human Services, 62. 200 Independence Ave SW ☎ 619-0257

Department of Housing & Urban Development, 82. 451 7th St SW ☎ 708-1422

Department of the Interior, 22. 1849 C St NW ☎ 208-3100

Department of Labor, 32. 200 Constitution Ave NW ☎ 219-6666

Department of Transportation, 83. 400 7th St SW ☎ 366-4000

Dirksen Senate Office Building, 53. 100 Constitution Ave NE ☎ 224-3121

Enid Haupt Memorial Garden, 71. 1050 Independence Ave SW ☎ 357-2700

Executive Office of the Mayor, 50. 44 4th St NW ☎ 727-2980

FBI, 39. 935 Pennsylvania Ave NW ☎ 324-3000

FDR Memorial, 13. Ohio Dr SW ☎ 426-6841

Federal Aviation Administration, 65. 800 Independence Ave SW ☎ 267-3484

Federal Reserve, 17. C & 20th St NW ☎ 452-3000

Federal Trade Commission, 34. Pennsylvania Ave and 6th St NW ☎ 326-2222

Folger Shakespeare Library, 56. 201 E Capitol St SE ☎ 544-4600

Ford's Theatre, 40. 517 10th St NW ☎ 426-6924

Freer Gallery, 74. Jefferson Dr & 12th St SW ☎ 357-4880

General Services Administration, 81. 700 D St SW ☎ 708-5082

Government Printing Office, 45. 732 N Capitol St NW ☎ 512-0000

Hart Senate Office Building, 53. 120 Constitution Ave NE ☎ 224-3121

Hirshhorn Museum, 66. Independence Ave & 7th St SW ☎ 357-2700

Internal Revenue Service, 37. 1111 Constitution Ave NW ☎ 622-2000

Interstate Commerce Commission, 27. 1200 Constitution Ave NW ☎ 358-7000

Jefferson Memorial, 80. W Potomac Park SW ☎ 426-6821

Justice Department, 36. 950 Pennsylvania Ave NW ☎ 514-2000

Kennedy Center, 8. New Hampshire Ave & Rock Creek Pkwy ☎ 467-4600

Korean War Veterans Memorial, 15. French Dr SW ☎ 426-6841

Library of Congress, 55. 10 First St SE ☎ 707-8000

Lincoln Memorial, 12. Constitution Ave and 23rd St SW ☎ 426-6841

National Academy of Sciences, 16. 2101 Constitution Ave NW ☎ 334-2000

National Aeronautics & Space Administration, 84. 300 E St SE ☎ 358-0000

Listed Alphabetically (cont.)

National Air & Space Museum, 64.
Independence Ave & 6th St SW
☎ 357-2700

National Archives, 35.
800 Constitution Ave NW ☎ 501-5000

National Building Museum, 50. 401
F St NW ☎ 272-2448

**National Capital Post Office and
Postal Museum, 46.** 2 Massachusetts
Ave NE ☎ 523-2628/633-9370

**National Gallery of Art (east wing),
31.** Constitution Ave & 4th St NW
☎ 737-4215

**National Gallery of Art (west wing),
30.** Constitution Ave & 6th St NW
☎ 737-4215

National Museum of African Art, 69.
950 Independence Ave SW
☎ 357-2700

**National Museum of American Art,
42.** G & 8th Sts NW ☎ 357-2700

**National Museum of American
History, 28.** Constitution Ave & 14th St
NW ☎ 357-2700

**National Museum of Natural
History, 29.** Constitution Ave &
10th St NW ☎ 357-2700

National Portrait Gallery, 41. F & 8th
Sts NW ☎ 357-2700

New Executive Office Building, 1.
725 17th St NW ☎ 395-3000

Octagon House, 19. 1799 New York
Ave NW ☎ 638-3105

Old Executive Office Building, 7.
1700 Pennsylvania Ave NW
☎ 395-3000

Old Post Office Pavilion, 38. 1100
Pennsylvania Ave NW ☎ 289-4224

**Organization of American
States, 23.** Constitution Ave &
17th St NW ☎ 458-3000

**Pan-American Health
Organization, 9.** 525 23rd St NW
☎ 974-3000

Rayburn House Office Building, 58.
50 Independence Ave SW
☎ 224-3121

Renwick Gallery, 2.
Pennsylvania Ave & 17th St NW
☎ 357-2700

Russell Senate Office Building, 52.
120 Constitution Ave NE ☎ 224-3121

Sackler Gallery, 75.
1050 Independence Ave SW
☎ 357-4880

Sculpture Gardens, 67.
Independence Ave & 8th St NW
☎ 357-2700

Smithsonian Castle, 70.
1000 Jefferson Dr SW ☎ 357-2700

State Dept., 10. 2201 C St NW
☎ 647-4000

Supreme Court, 54. 1 First St NE
☎ 479-3000

Sylvan Theater, 77. Independence
Ave & 15th St SW ☎ 426-6841

Treasury, 5. Pennsylvania Ave & 15th St
NW ☎ 622-2000

Union Station, 47. 50 Massachusetts
Ave NE ☎ 371-9441

US Botanic Gardens, 60. Maryland
Ave & First St SW ☎ 225-8333

US Capitol, 59.
Capitol St ☎ 224-3121

US Courthouse, 33. 333 Constitution
Ave NW ☎ 273-0300

**US Holocaust Memorial
Museum, 78.** 200 Raoul Wallenberg
Pl SW ☎ 488-0400

US Tax Court, 51. 400 2nd St NW
☎ 606-8754

Vietnam Veterans Memorial, 14.
Constitution Ave & 21st St NW
☎ 426-6841

Vietnam Women's Memorial, 11.
Constitution Gardens, Constitution Ave
& 23rd St NW ☎ 426-6841

Voice of America, 61. 330
Independence Ave SW ☎ 619-4700

Washington Monument, 76.
The Mall & 15th St NW ☎ 426-6841

White House, 6.
1600 Pennsylvania Ave NW
☎ 456-7041

MAP 23 The White House

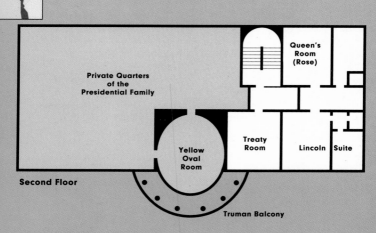

Private Quarters of the Presidential Family

Queen's Room (Rose)

Treaty Room

Lincoln Suite

Yellow Oval Room

Second Floor

Truman Balcony

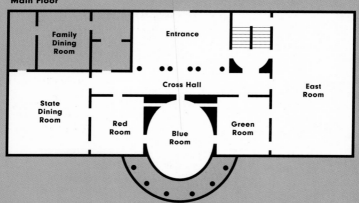

Main Floor

Family Dining Room

Entrance

State Dining Room

Cross Hall

East Room

Red Room

Blue Room

Green Room

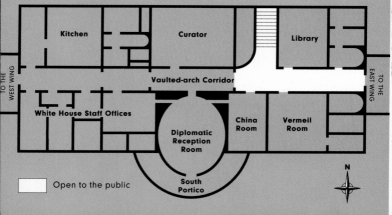

Ground Floor

Kitchen

Curator

Library

TO THE WEST WING

Vaulted-arch Corridor

TO THE EAST WING

White House Staff Offices

Diplomatic Reception Room

China Room

Vermeil Room

South Portico

Open to the public

N

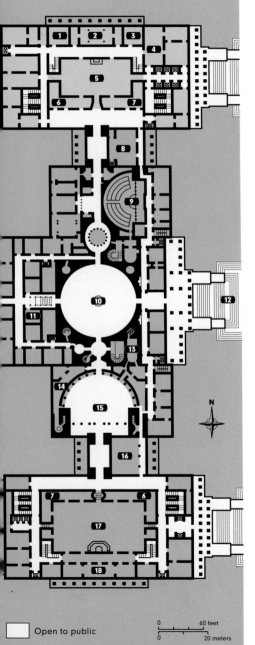

N

Open to public

0   60 feet
0   20 meters

Listed Alphabetically

African Art (Nat'l Mus), 41.
950 Independence Ave SW
☎ 357-2700

Air & Space (National Museum), 44.
Independence Ave & 6th St SW
☎ 357-2700

American Art (National Museum), 24.
G & 8th Sts NW ☎ 357-2700

American History (National Museum), 33. Constitution Ave & 14th St NW ☎ 357-2700

Anacostia, 48.
1901 Fort Pl SE ☎ 357-1300

Arts and Industries, 42.
900 Jefferson Dr SW ☎ 357-2700

Bethune, 13.
1318 Vermont Ave NW ☎ 332-1233

Black Fashion, 14.
2007 Vermont Ave NW ☎ 667-0744

Bureau of Engraving & Printing, 47.
1400 C St SW ☎ 622-2000

Corcoran Gallery, 23.
New York Ave & 17th St NW ☎ 639-1700

DAR, 30. 1776 D St NW ☎ 879-3254

Decatur House, 16. 748 Jackson Pl NW
☎ 842-0920

Department of the Interior, 29.
1849 C St NW ☎ 208-3100

Dolls' House & Toy, 3.
5236 44th St NW ☎ 244-0024

Dumbarton Oaks, 8.
1703 32nd St NW ☎ 339-6401

FBI, 27. 950 Pennsylvania Ave NW
☎ 324-3000

Ford's Theatre, 26. 511 10th St NW
☎ 426-6924

Frederick Douglass Nat'l Historic Site, 49. 1411 W St SE ☎ 426-5961

Hillwood, 2. 4155 Linnean Ave NW
☎ 686-5807

Hirshhorn, 43. Independence Ave & 7th St SW ☎ 357-2700

Jewish Historical Society, 18.
701 3rd St NW ☎ 789-0900

Jewish Military History and Memorial, 10. 1811 R St NW
☎ 265-6280

Library of Congress, 38.
10 First St SE ☎ 707-8000

Marine Corps, 50.
Navy Yard, 901 M St SE ☎ 433-3340

Meridian House, 7. 1624 Crescent Pl NW ☎ 667-6800

Museum of the Americas, 31. 201 18th St NW ☎ 458-6016

Nat'l Aquarium, 32. Constitution Ave & 14th St NW ☎ 482-2825

Nat'l Archives, 35. 800 Constitution Ave NW ☎ 501-5000

National Building, 28. 401 F St NW
☎ 272-2448

Nat'l Gallery of Art, 36. Constitution Ave & 6th St NW ☎ 737-4215

National Geographic, 12.
M & 17th Sts NW ☎ 857-7588

National Jewish Museum, 11.
1640 Rhode Island Ave NW ☎ 857-6583

National Learning Center, 19.
800 3rd St NE ☎ 543-8600

National Portrait Gallery, 25.
F & 8th Sts NW ☎ 357-2700

National Postal Museum, 20. 2 Massachusetts Ave NE ☎ 633-9370

National Zoo, 1. 3001 Connecticut Ave NW ☎ 673-4800

Natural History (National Museum), 34. Constitution Ave & 10th St NW
☎ 357-2700

Naval Observatory, 4. Massachusetts Ave & 34th St NW ☎ 653-1507

Navy, 51. Navy Yard, 901 M St SE
☎ 433-4882

Octagon House, 21. 1799 New York Ave NW ☎ 638-3105

Phillips Collection, 9.
1600 21st St NW ☎ 387-2151

Renwick Gallery, 15. Pennsylvania Ave & 17th St NW ☎ 357-1300

Sackler Gallery, 40. 1050 Independence Ave SW ☎ 357-4880

Smithsonian Institution (Info Ctr), 39.
1000 Jefferson Dr NW ☎ 357-2700

Textile, 5. 2320 S St NW ☎ 667-0441

US Botanic Gardens, 45. Maryland Ave & 1st St SW ☎ 225-8333

US Capitol, 37. Capitol St ☎ 224-3121

US Holocaust Memorial, 46. 200 Raoul Wallenberg Pl SW ☎ 488-0400

White House, 22. 1600 Pennsylvania Ave NW ☎ 456-7041

Women in Arts (National Museum), 17.
1250 New York Ave NW ☎ 783-5000

Woodrow Wilson House, 6.
2340 S St NW ☎ 387-4062

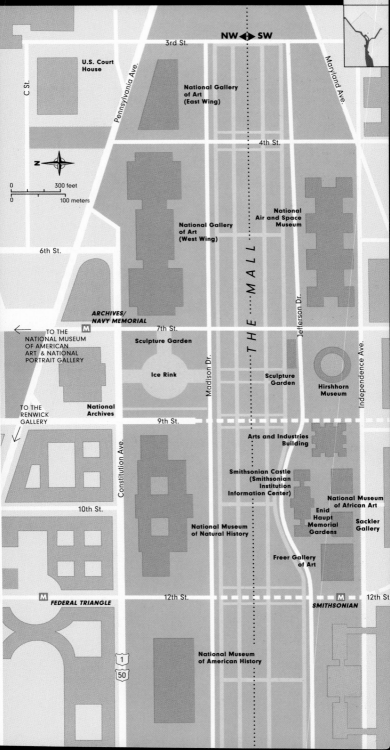

NW ◆ SW

3rd St.

U.S. Court House

National Gallery of Art (East Wing)

C St.

Pennsylvania Ave.

Maryland Ave.

4th St.

N

0   300 feet
0   100 meters

National Gallery of Art (West Wing)

National Air and Space Museum

6th St.

Jefferson Dr.

T H E · · · M A L L

ARCHIVES/ NAVY MEMORIAL

TO THE NATIONAL MUSEUM OF AMERICAN ART & NATIONAL PORTRAIT GALLERY

7th St.

Sculpture Garden

Ice Rink

Madison Dr.

Sculpture Garden

Hirshhorn Museum

Independence Ave.

TO THE RENWICK GALLERY

National Archives

9th St.

Arts and Industries Building

Constitution Ave.

Smithsonian Castle (Smithsonian Institution Information Center)

National Museum of African Art

Enid Haupt Memorial Gardens

Sackler Gallery

10th St.

National Museum of Natural History

Freer Gallery of Art

FEDERAL TRIANGLE

12th St.

12th St.

SMITHSONIAN

1
50

National Museum of American History

MAP 27 National Gallery of Art/West Wing

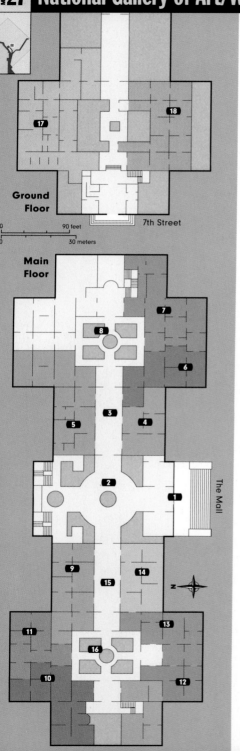

Ground Floor

90 feet

30 meters

7th Street

Main Floor

The Mall

National Air & Space Museum

MAP 28

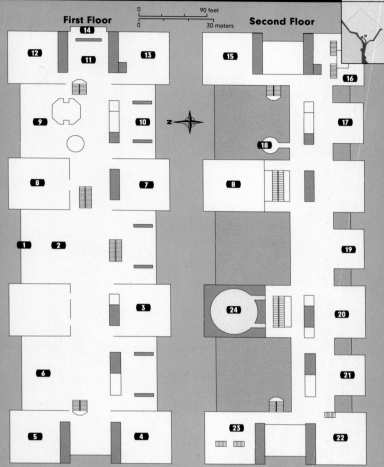

First Floor Second Floor

0 — 90 feet
0 — 30 meters

Listed by Site Number

MAP 29 Exploring Georgetown

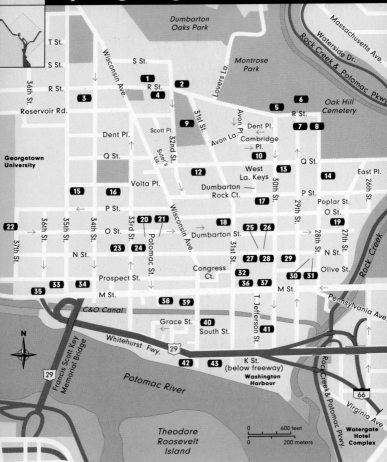

Dumbarton Oaks Park

Montrose Park

Massachusetts Ave

Waterside Dr.

Rock Creek & Potomac Pkwy

T St.

S St.

R St.

Reservoir Rd.

36th St.

Wisconsin Ave.

S St.

R St.

Lovers La.

Oak Hill Cemetery

Dent Pl.

Scott Pl.

31st St.

Avon Pl.

Avon La.

Dent Pl.

Cambridge Pl.

Georgetown University

Q St.

32nd St.

Suter's La.

West La. Keys

Dumbarton Rock Ct.

Q St.

East Pl.

26th St.

Volta Pl.

Wisconsin Ave.

30th St.

P St.

Poplar St.

O St.

29th St.

28th St.

27th St.

Rock Creek

P St.

36th St.

35th St.

34th St.

33rd St.

Potomac St.

O St.

Dumbarton St.

31st St.

N St.

Olive St.

37th St.

N St.

Congress Ct.

T. Jefferson St.

M St.

Pennsylvania Ave.

Prospect St.

M St.

C&O Canal

Francis Scott Key Memorial Bridge

Whitehurst Fwy.

Grace St.

South St.

29

Rock Creek & Potomac Pkwy

Potomac River

K St. (below freeway)

Washington Harbour

66

Virginia Ave.

Watergate Hotel Complex

Theodore Roosevelt Island

N

600 feet

200 meters

Listed by Site Number

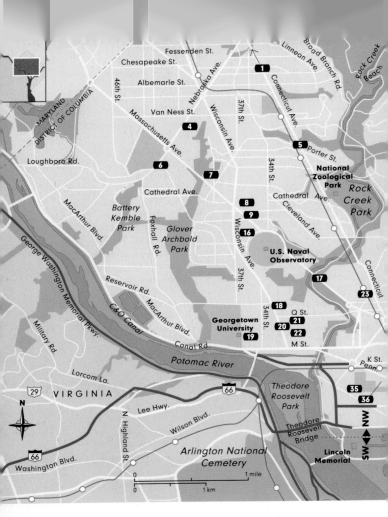

Listed by Site Number

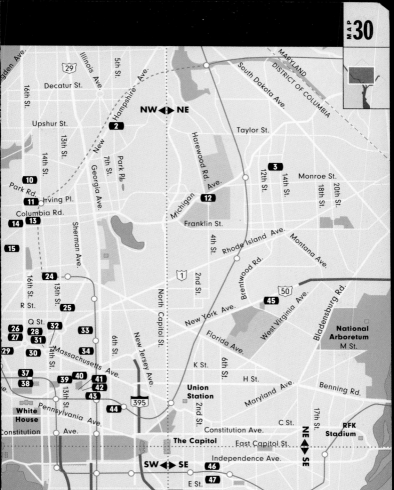

MAP 30

Listed by Site Number (cont.)

Listed Alphabetically

Adas Israel Synagogue, 5.
2850 Quebec St NW
☎ 362-4433. Conservative

All Souls Unitarian, 14.
2835 16th St NW ☎ 332-5266

Asbury Methodist, 40.
926 11th St NW ☎ 628-0009

Calvary Baptist, 43.
755 8th St NW ☎ 347-8355

Capitol Hill Presbyterian, 46.
201 4th St SE ☎ 547-8676

Cathedral of St Sophia, 9.
Mass Ave & 36th St NW ☎ 333-4730.
Greek Orthodox

Central Presbyterian, 11.
Irving Pl & 15th St NW (site only)

Christ Church, 48.
620 G St SE ☎ 547-9300. Episcopal

Church of Jesus Christ of Latter-Day Saints, 1. 1000 Stonybrook Dr,
Kensington, MD ☎ 301/589-0144.
Mormon

Church of the Epiphany, 39.
1317 G St NW ☎ 347-2635. Episcopal

Ebenezer United Methodist, 47.
400 D St SE ☎ 544-9539

First Baptist, 27. 1328 16th St NW
☎ 387-2206

First Church of Christ, Scientist, 15.
1770 Euclid St NW ☎ 265-1390

First Congregational, 42. 945 G St
NW ☎ 628-4317. United Church of Christ

Foundry United Methodist, 26.
1500 16th St NW ☎ 332-4010

Franciscan Monastery, 3. 1400 Quincy
St NE ☎ 526-6800. Roman Catholic

Friends Meeting of Washington, 23.
2111 Florida Ave NW ☎ 483-3310. Quaker

Georgetown Lutheran, 18.
1556 Wisconsin Ave NW ☎ 337-9070

Grace Reformed, 28. 1405 15th St NW
☎ 387-3131. United Church of Christ

Holy Trinity, 19. 3513 N St NW
☎ 337-2840. Roman Catholic

Islamic Center Mosque, 17. 2551
Massachusetts Ave NW ☎ 332-8343

Kesher Israel, 21. 2801 N St NW
☎ 333-4808. Orthodox

Luther Place Memorial, 32. 1226
Vermont Ave NW ☎ 667-1377. Lutheran

**Metropolitan African Methodist
Episcopal, 30.** 1518 M St NW ☎ 331-1426

Metropolitan Baptist, 25. 1225 R St
NW ☎ 483-1540

Metro Memorial United Methodist, 6.
3401 Nebraska Ave NW ☎ 363-4900

**Mt Vernon Place United
Methodist, 34.** 900 Massachusetts
Ave NW ☎ 347-9620

Mt Zion United Methodist, 22.
1334 29th St NW ☎ 234-0148

National Baptist Memorial, 13.
1501 Columbia Rd NW ☎ 265-1410

National City Christian, 31. 5 Thomas
Circle NW ☎ 232-0323. Disciples of Christ

National Presbyterian, 4.
4101 Nebraska Ave NW ☎ 537-0800

**National Shrine of the Immaculate
Conception, 12.** Michigan Ave & 4th
St NE ☎ 526-8300. Roman Catholic

New York Ave Presbyterian, 45.
1313 New York Ave NW ☎ 393-3700

Shiloh Baptist, 33. 1500 9th St NW
☎ 232-4200

St Augustine, 24. 1419 V St NW
☎ 265-1470. Roman Catholic

St John's Episcopal, 38.
1525 H St NW ☎ 347-8766

**St John's Episcopal (Georgetown),
20.** 3240 O St NW ☎ 338-1796.

St Mary's Catholic, 44.
727 5th St NW ☎ 289-7770

St Mary's Episcopal, 35.
728 23rd St NW ☎ 333-3985

St Matthew's Cathedral, 29.
1725 Rhode Is Ave NW ☎ 347-3215.
Roman Catholic

St Patrick's, 41. 619 10th St NW
☎ 347-2713. Roman Catholic

St Paul's Rock Creek, 2.
Rock Creek Church Rd & Webster St NW
☎ 726-2080. Episcopal

St Stephen Church, 10. 1525 Newton
St NW ☎ 232-0900. Episcopal

Temple Micah, 16. 2829 Wisconsin
Ave NW ☎ 342-9175. Reform

Third Church of Christ, Scientist, 37.
900 16th St NW ☎ 833-3325

Wash Hebrew Congregation, 7. 3935
Macomb St NW ☎ 362-7100. Reform

Washington National Cathedral, 8.
Wisconsin & Mass Aves NW
☎ 537-6200. Episcopal

Western Presbyterian, 36.
2401 Virginia Ave NW ☎ 835-8383

Listed Alphabetically

Listed by Site Number (cont.)

Wythe St.

Pendleton St.

1
2 **3**

Oronoco St.

Princess St.

4

Queen St.

5

6

7

13

Cameron St.

16
17

15

West St.

Payne St.

Fayette St.

Henry St.

Patrick St.

Alfred St.

Columbus St.

Washington St.

St. Asaph St.

Pitt St.

Royal St.

Fairfax St.

Lee St.

Union St.

Potomac River

8

King St.

9

10

11

12

19 **20**
18

14

Prince St.

22

21

N

Duke St.

23 **24**

25

Wolfe St.

0   600 feet
0   200 meters

Listed by Site Number

1 Robert E Lee House
2 Edmund Jennings Lee House
3 Fendall-John L Lewis House
4 Brockett's Row
5 Lloyd House
6 Yeaton-Fairfax House
7 Christ Church
8 George Washington Masonic Nat'l Mem
9 Friendship Fire Co
10 William Fowle House
11 Lyceum
12 Lloyd's Row
13 Gadsby's Tavern Museum
14 Gentry Row
15 Torpedo Factory Arts Center
16 Carlyle House
17 Ramsay House
18 Stabler-Leadbeater Apothecary Shop
19 Thompson-Marshburn House
20 Athenaeum
21 Captain's Row
22 Dr Wm Brown House
23 St Mary's Church
24 Dr James Craik House
25 Old Presbyterian Meeting House

Listed Alphabetically

Athenaeum, 20. 201 Prince St

Brockett's Row, 4. 301-7 N Washington St

Captain's Row, 21. Prince St

Carlyle House, 16. 121 N Fairfax St

Christ Church, 7. 118 N Washington St

Dr James Craik House, 24. 210 Duke St

Dr William Brown House, 22. 212 S Fairfax St

Edmund Jennings Lee House, 2. Oronoco & N Washington Sts

Fendall-John L Lewis House, 3. 614 Oronoco St

Friendship Fire Co, 9. 107 S Alfred St

Gadsby's Tavern Museum, 13. 134-138 N Royal St

Gentry Row, 14. Prince St

George Washington Masonic National Memorial, 8. 101 Callahan Dr

Lloyd House, 5. Queen & N Washington Sts

Lloyd's Row, 12. 220-228 S Washington St

Lyceum, 11. 201 S Washington St

Old Presbyterian Meeting House, 25. 321 S Fairfax St

Ramsay House (Visitor's Center), 17. King & N Fairfax Sts

Robert E Lee House, 1. 607 Oronoco St

St Mary's Church, 23. 310 Duke St

Stabler-Leadbeater Apothecary Shop, 18. 105-107 S Fairfax St

Thompson-Marshburn House, 19. 211 N Fairfax St

Torpedo Factory Arts Center, 15. 105 N Union St

William Fowle House, 10. 711 Prince St

Yeaton-Fairfax House, 6. 607 Cameron St

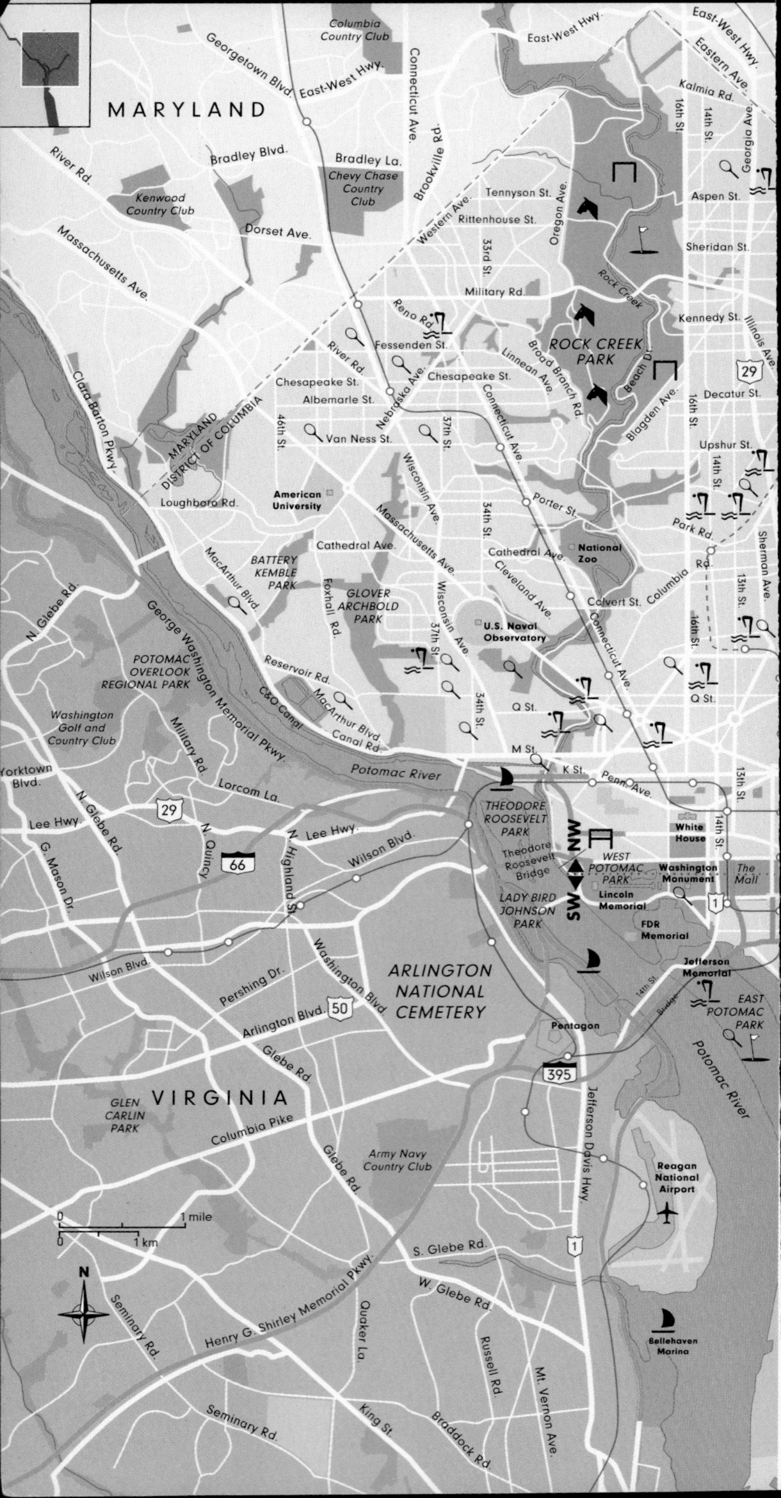
MARYLAND
VIRGINIA
DISTRICT OF COLUMBIA
Columbia Country Club
Chevy Chase Country Club
Kenwood Country Club
ROCK CREEK PARK
National Zoo
American University
BATTERY KEMBLE PARK
GLOVER ARCHBOLD PARK
U.S. Naval Observatory
POTOMAC OVERLOOK REGIONAL PARK
Washington Golf and Country Club
THEODORE ROOSEVELT PARK
Theodore Roosevelt Bridge
WEST POTOMAC PARK
LADY BIRD JOHNSON PARK
White House
Washington Monument
The Mall
Lincoln Memorial
FDR Memorial
Jefferson Memorial
EAST POTOMAC PARK
ARLINGTON NATIONAL CEMETERY
Pentagon
GLEN CARLIN PARK
Army Navy Country Club
Reagan National Airport
Bellehaven Marina
Potomac River
C&O Canal
Rock Creek
Georgetown Blvd.
East-West Hwy.
Connecticut Ave.
Brookville Rd.
Bradley Blvd.
Bradley La.
River Rd.
Dorset Ave.
Massachusetts Ave.
Western Ave.
Tennyson St.
Rittenhouse St.
Oregon Ave.
33rd St.
Military Rd.
Reno Rd.
Fessenden St.
Chesapeake St.
Albemarle St.
Van Ness St.
46th St.
37th St.
Nebraska Ave.
Wisconsin Ave.
Linnean Ave.
Broad Branch Rd.
Beach Dr.
Blagden Ave.
Kalmia Rd.
Eastern Ave.
16th St.
14th St.
Georgia Ave.
Aspen St.
Sheridan St.
Kennedy St.
Illinois Ave.
Decatur St.
Upshur St.
Park Rd.
Sherman Ave.
Columbia Rd.
13th St.
Porter St.
Cathedral Ave.
34th St.
Cleveland Ave.
Calvert St.
Clara Barton Pkwy.
Loughboro Rd.
MacArthur Blvd.
Foxhall Rd.
Reservoir Rd.
Canal Rd.
Q St.
M St.
K St.
Penn. Ave.
George Washington Memorial Pkwy.
N. Glebe Rd.
Military Rd.
Yorktown Blvd.
Lorcom La.
Lee Hwy.
N. Quincy
N. Highland St.
Wilson Blvd.
G. Mason Dr.
Washington Blvd.
Pershing Dr.
Arlington Blvd.
Glebe Rd.
Columbia Pike
Jefferson Davis Hwy.
14th St. Bridge
S. Glebe Rd.
W. Glebe Rd.
Henry G. Shirley Memorial Pkwy.
Quaker La.
Seminary Rd.
Russell Rd.
Mt. Vernon Ave.
King St.
Braddock Rd.
29
66
50
395
1
NW
SW
0
1 mile
0
1 km
N

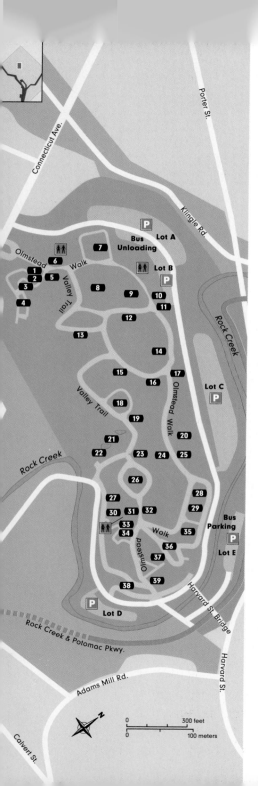

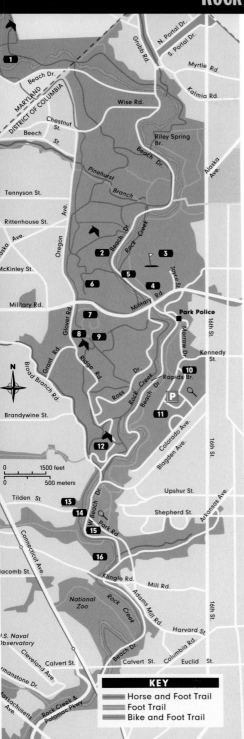

KEY

Horse and Foot Trail
Foot Trail
Bike and Foot Trail

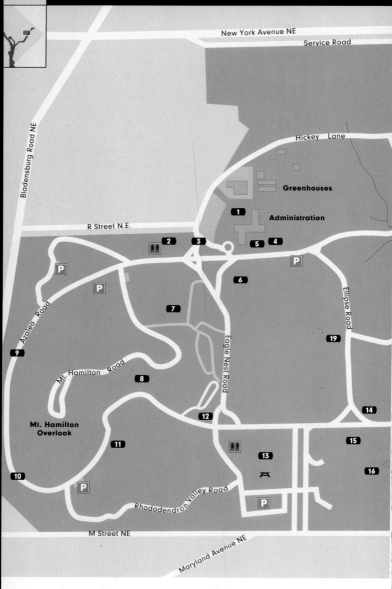

MAP 37

New York Avenue NE

Service Road

Hickey Lane

Greenhouses

1

Administration

R Street N.E.

2 **3**

5 **4**

6

Bladensburg Road NE

Azalea Road

P

P

7

9

Mt. Hamilton Road

8

Eagle Nest Road

Ellipse Road

19

12

14

Mt. Hamilton Overlook

11

13

15

10

16

Rhododendron Valley Road

P

M Street NE

Maryland Avenue NE

Listed by Site Number

1 Court of Honor	**8** Azalea Hillside	**15** Shade Trees
2 Information Center	**9** Crab Apples	**16** Shade Trees
3 Friendship Garden	**10** Viburnum	**17** Washington Youth Garden
4 Bonsai and Penjing Collection	**11** Azalea Valley	**18** Fern Valley
5 Aquatic Gardens	**12** Morrison Azalea Garden	**19** National Capitol Columns
6 Herb Garden	**13** State Trees	**20** Beech Pond Gazebo
7 Lee Azalea Garden	**14** Native Plants	

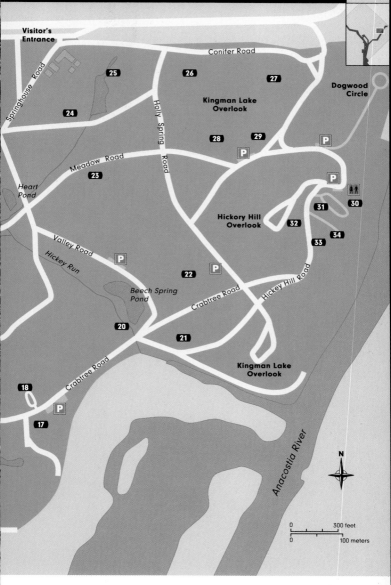

MAP 37

Visitor's Entrance

Conifer Road

25

26

27

Dogwood Circle

Springhouse Road

24

Kingman Lake Overlook

Holly Spring Road

28

29

P

P

Meadow Road

23

Heart Pond

P

Hickory Hill Overlook

31

30

32

34

33

Valley Road

P

Hickey Run

22

P

Hickory Hill Road

Beech Spring Pond

Crabtree Road

20

21

Kingman Lake Overlook

18

Crabtree Road

P

17

Anacostia River

N

0   300 feet

0   100 meters

MAP 38 Biking Trails

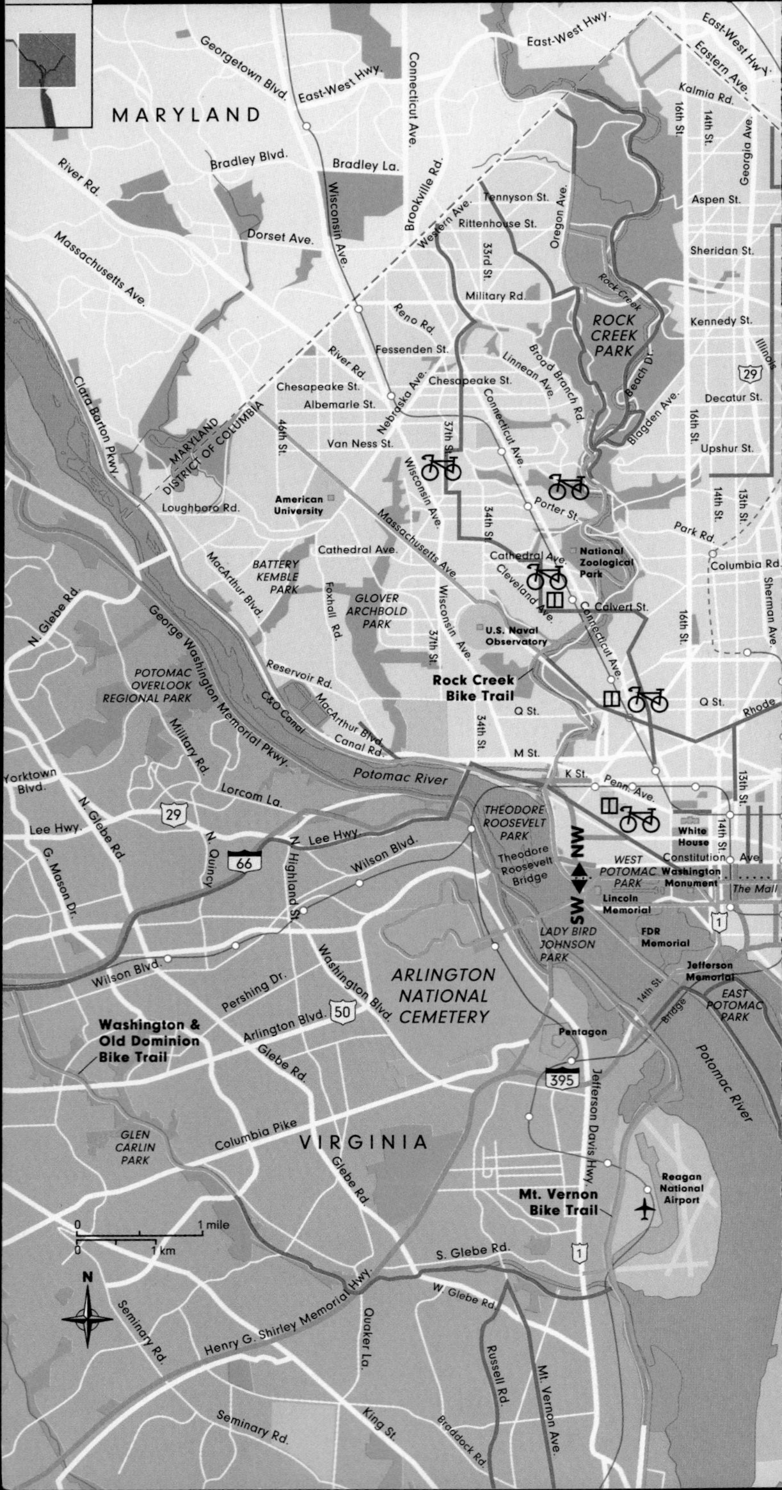

MARYLAND

Georgetown Blvd.
East-West Hwy.
East-West Hwy.
Eastern Ave.
16th St.
Kalmia Rd.
14th St.
Georgia Ave.
Aspen St.

Bradley Blvd.
Bradley La.
Connecticut Ave.
Wisconsin Ave.
Brookville Rd.
Western Ave.
Tennyson St.
Rittenhouse St.
33rd St.
Oregon Ave.
Sheridan St.

River Rd.
Dorset Ave.
Massachusetts Ave.
Military Rd.
Rock Creek
Kennedy St.

ROCK CREEK PARK

Clara Barton Pkwy.
River Rd.
Reno Rd.
Fessenden St.
Nebraska Ave.
Chesapeake St.
Linnean Ave.
Broad Branch Rd.
Beech Dr.
Blagden Ave.
Decatur St.
16th St.
Upshur St.
29

MARYLAND
DISTRICT OF COLUMBIA
Loughboro Rd.
4th St.
Albemarle St.
Van Ness St.
37th St.
Wisconsin Ave.
34th St.
Connecticut Ave.
Porter St.
Park Rd.
Columbia Rd.
13th St.
Sherman Ave.

American University
BATTERY KEMBLE PARK
Cathedral Ave.
Massachusetts Ave.
Cathedral Ave.
Cleveland Ave.
National Zoological Park
Calvert St.

MacArthur Blvd.
Foxhall Rd.
GLOVER ARCHBOLD PARK
37th St.
Wisconsin Ave.
34th St.
U.S. Naval Observatory

N. Glebe Rd.
POTOMAC OVERLOOK REGIONAL PARK
George Washington Memorial Pkwy.
Reservoir Rd.
C&O Canal
MacArthur Blvd.
Canal Rd.
Rock Creek Bike Trail
Q St.
Q St.
Rhode

Military Rd.
Lorcom La.
Potomac River
M St.
K St.
Penn. Ave.
13th St.

Yorktown Blvd.
N. Glebe Rd.
Lee Hwy.
29
G. Mason Dr.
N. Quincy St.
66
N. Highland St.
N. Lee Hwy.
Wilson Blvd.
THEODORE ROOSEVELT PARK
Theodore Roosevelt Bridge
WEST POTOMAC PARK
White House
Constitution Ave.
Washington Monument
The Mall
1

Wilson Blvd.
Pershing Dr.
Washington Blvd.
Arlington Blvd.
50
Glebe Rd.
ARLINGTON NATIONAL CEMETERY
LADY BIRD JOHNSON PARK
Lincoln Memorial
FDR Memorial
Jefferson Memorial
EAST POTOMAC PARK

Washington & Old Dominion Bike Trail
Columbia Pike
GLEN CARLIN PARK
VIRGINIA
Glebe Rd.
Pentagon
395
Jefferson Davis Hwy.
Potomac River

Mt. Vernon Bike Trail
Reagan National Airport

Seminary Rd.
Henry G. Shirley Memorial Hwy.
S. Glebe Rd.
W. Glebe Rd.
Quaker La.
1

N
Seminary Rd.
King St.
Russell Rd.
Mt. Vernon Ave.
Braddock Rd.

0   1 mile
0   1 km

Swains Lock (Lock 21)

SEE DETAIL MAP OPPOSITE

Great Falls Park Visitor Center

Great Falls Tavern Visitor Center

Great Falls Park

Falls Rd.

189

River Rd.

Old Dominion Dr.

Maryland Gold Mine site

190

Old Angler's Inn

P

MacArthur Blvd.

MARYLAND

738

193

Carderock

495

Capital Beltway

Washington Dulles Access and Toll Rd.

Old Georgetown Pike

495

Lock 14

Lock 13 · Lock 12

Lock 11

P

Seven Locks

Lock 10
Lock 9
Lock 8

P

George Washington Memorial Parkway

267

Dolley

Madison Blvd.

123

George Washington Memorial Pkwy.

Lock 7

P

396

McLEAN

Chain Bridge Rd.

BETHESDA

VIRGINIA

Little Falls Dam

309

Lock 6

P

Lock 5

River Rd.

Little Falls

Lee Hwy.

ARLINGTON

Chain Bridge

Canal Rd.

Massachusetts Ave.

Wisconsin Ave.

29

Abner Cloud House

Fletcher's Boathouse

MacArthur Blvd.

DISTRICT OF COLUMBIA

66

Lee Hwy.

Lee Hwy.

50

Potomac River

Rock Creek Park

GEORGETOWN

Key Bridge

Locks 1–4

16th St.

Arlington Blvd

50

New Hampshire Ave.

27

0   1 mile
0   1 km

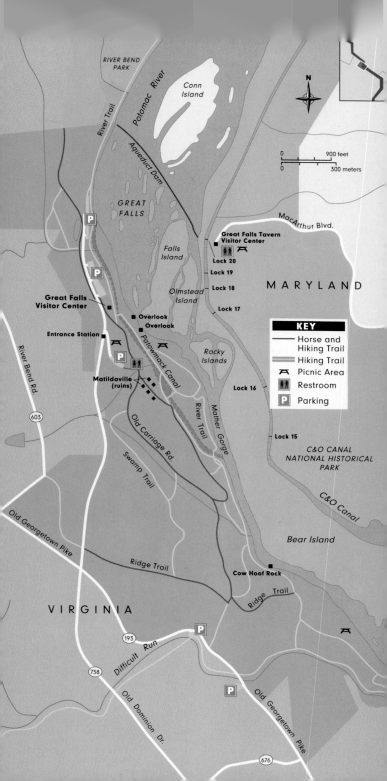

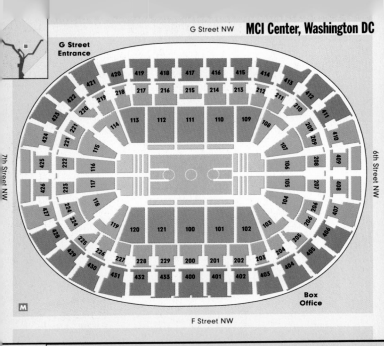

MCI Center, Washington DC

G Street NW

G Street Entrance

7th Street NW

6th Street NW

Box Office

F Street NW

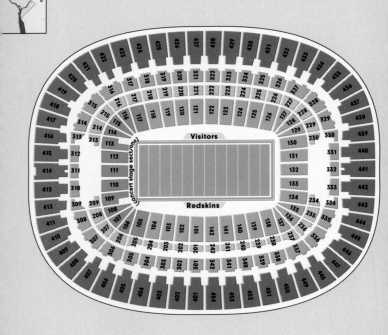

Jack Kent Cooke Stadium, Landover MD

Visitors

Redskins

(concert stage sections)

Oriole Park at Camden Yards, Baltimore MD

CLUB LEVEL
TERRACE BOXES
LOWER BOXES
Pressbox
Dugout
Dugout
RESERVED LOWER
Bull pens
Out-of-Town Scoreboard
BLEACHERS
Videoboard and Game Scoreboard

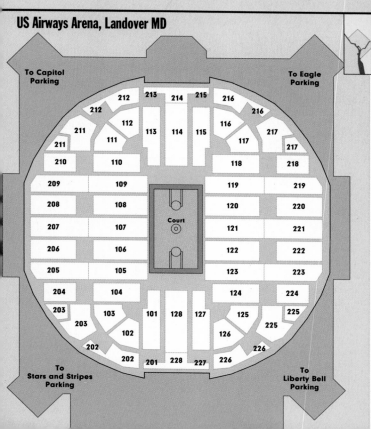

US Airways Arena, Landover MD

To Capitol Parking

To Eagle Parking

Court

To Stars and Stripes Parking

To Liberty Bell Parking

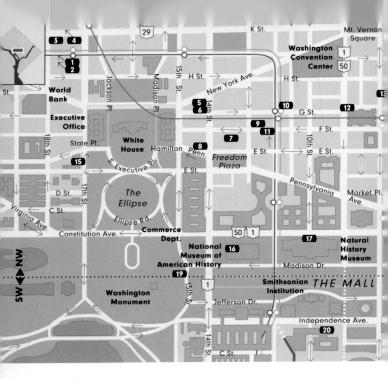

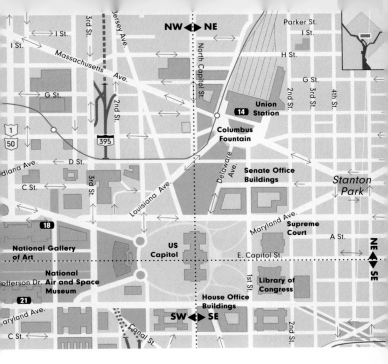

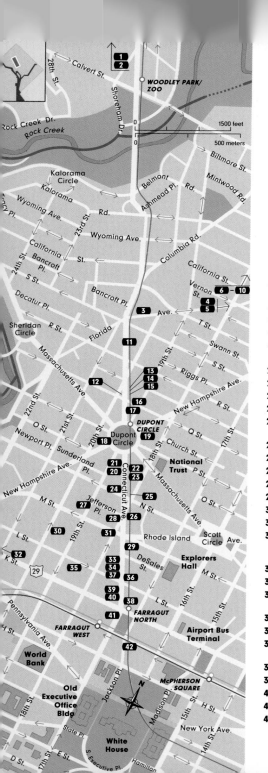

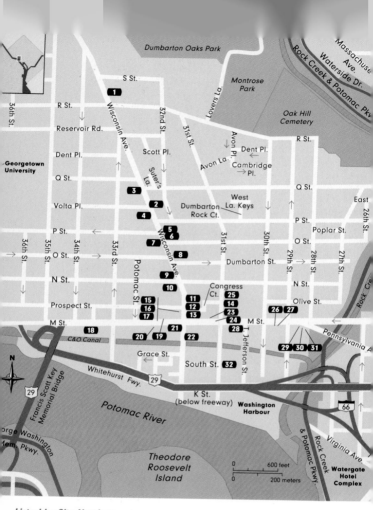

Listed Alphabetically

Ballston Commons, 16.
☎ 703/243-8088

Chevy Chase Pavilion, 5.
☎ 686-5335

City Place, 4. ☎ 301/589-1091

Dupont Circle Area, 9.

Eastern Market, 14.

Fair Oaks Mall, 20. ☎ 703/359-8300

Fashion Center, 15. ☎ 703/415-2400

Galleria at Tyson's II, 18.
☎ 703/827-7700

Georgetown Park, 10. ☎ 298-5577

Lake Forest Mall, 1.
☎ 301/840-5840

Landmark Center, 21.
☎ 703/941-2582

Landover Mall, 8.
☎ 301/341-3200

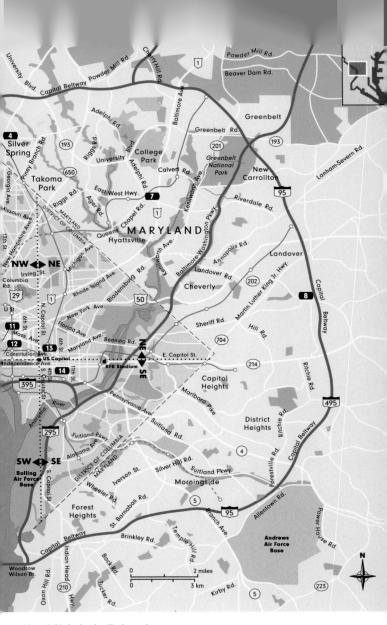

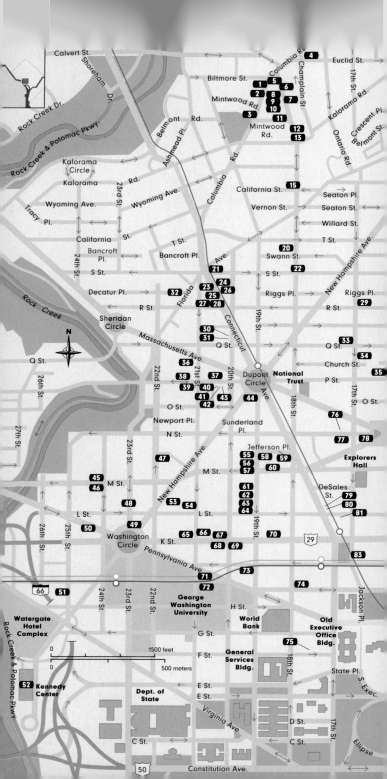

Listed by Site Number

MAP 46

Listed Alphabetically

Addis Ababa, 15. 2106 18th St NW
☎ 232-6092. Ethiopian. $$$

Anna Maria's, 24.
1737 Connecticut Ave NW
☎ 667-1444. Italian. $$

Ascot, 81. 1708 L St NW
☎ 296-7640. Continental. $$

Austin Grill, 118. 750 E St NW
☎ 393-3776. Tex-Mex. $$

Bacchus, 59. 1827 Jefferson Plaza NW
☎ 785-0734. Middle Eastern. $$

Be Du Ci, 39. 2100 P NW
☎ 223-3824. Mediterranean. $$$

Belmont Kitchen, 11. 2400 18th St NW
☎ 667-1200. American. $$

BenKay, 90. 727 15th St NW
☎ 737-1515. Japanese. $

Ben's Chili Bowl, 19. 1213 U St NW
☎ 667-0909. American. $

Bice, 121. 601 Pennsylvania Ave NW
☎ 638-2423. Italian. $$$$

Blackie's House of Beef, 47.
1217 22nd St NW ☎ 333-1100.
American. $$

Blossoms, 105.
Old Post Office Pavilion NW
☎ 371-1838. American. $$

Bombay Club, 83.
815 Connecticut Ave NW
☎ 659-3727. Indian. $$

Bristol Grill, 50. 2430 Pennsylvania
Ave NW ☎ 955-6400. American. $$$

Cafe Asia, 62. 1134 19th St NW
☎ 659-2696. Asian. $

Café Atlántico, 117. 405 8th St NW
☎ 393-0812. New Latin. $$$

Cafe Japone, 40. 2032 P St NW
☎ 223-1573. Japanese. $$-$$$

Cafe Luna, 35. 1633 P St NW
☎ 387-4005. American. $

Cafe Mozart, 92. 1331 H St NW
☎ 347-5732. German. $

Cafe Petitto, 25.
1724 Connecticut Ave NW
☎ 462-8771. Italian. $

Cafe Promenade, 79.
1127 Connecticut Ave NW
☎ 347-8900. Mediterranean. $$

Capital City Brewing Co, 95.
1100 New York Ave NW
☎ 628-2222. American. $$

Cashion's Eats Place, 1.
1819 Columbia Rd NW
☎ 393-0812. Caribbean. $$

Charlie Chiang's, 73. 1912 I St NW
☎ 293-6000. Chinese. $$

Charlie's Crab, 80.
1101 Connecticut Ave NW
☎ 785-4505. Seafood. $$

Childe Harold, 30. 1610 20th St NW
☎ 483-6702. American. $$

China Inn, 108. 631 H St NW
☎ 842-0909. Chinese. $$

Churerria Madrid, 4. 2505
Champlain St NW ☎ 483-4441.
Spanish. $

Cities, 9. 2424 18th St NW
☎ 328-2100. Continental. $$$

City Lights of China, 26. 1731
Connecticut Ave NW ☎ 265-6688.
Chinese. $

Coco Loco, 111. 810 7th St NW
☎ 289-2626. Brazilian. $$

Coeur de Lion, 94.
926 Massachusetts Ave NW
☎ 414-0500. Continental. $$$

The Colonnade, 45. 2401 M St NW
☎ 429-2400. Continental. $$$$

Coppi's Restaurant, 17. 1414 U St NW
☎ 319-7773. Italian. $$-$$$

El Catalan, 101. 1319 F St NW
☎ 628-2299. Spanish. $$$

Felix, 10. 2406 18th St NW
☎ 483-3549. New American. $$$

Florida Ave Grill, 14. 1100 Florida
Ave NW ☎ 265-1586. Soul Food. $

Foggy Bottom Café, 51. 924 25th St
NW ☎ 338-8707. American. $$

Food for Thought, 23.
1738 Connecticut Ave NW
☎ 797-1095. Vegetarian.

Fran O'Brien's Steak House, 82.
1001 16th St ☎ 783-2599.
American. $$$

Friday's, 103.
1201 Pennsylvania Ave NW
☎ 628-8443. American. $

Front Page, 44. 1333 New Hampshire
Ave NW ☎ 296-6500. American. $$

Gabriel, 38. 2121 P St NW
☎ 822-8157. Spanish. $$$

$$$$ = over $35 $$$ = $25-$35 $$ = $15-$25 $ = under $15
Based on cost per person, excluding drinks, service, and 9% sales tax.

MAP 46 **Dining/Downtown**

Listed Alphabetically (cont.)

Galileo, 54. 1110 21st St NW
☎ 293-7191. Italian. $$$

Georgia Brown's, 86. 950 15th St NW ☎ 393-4499. Southern. $$

Gerard's Place, 85. 915 15th St NW
☎ 737-4445. French. $$$

Ginza Japanese, 66. 1009 21st St NW
☎ 833-1244. Japanese. $$

Golden Palace, 115. 720 7th St NW
☎ 783-1225. Chinese. $$

Goldoni, 48. 1113 23rd St NW
☎ 293-1511. Italian. $$

Grill from Ipanema, 3.
1858 Columbia Rd ☎ 986-0757.
Brazilian. $$

Gusti's, 60. 1837 M St NW
☎ 331-9444. Italian. $$

Haad Thai, 95.
1100 New York Ave NW
☎ 682-1111. Thai. $$

Hard Rock Cafe, 116. 999 E St NW
☎ 737-7625. American. $$

Harvest Veranda, 88. 1400 M St NW
☎ 429-1700. American. $$$$

Herb's Restaurant, 78.
1615 Rhode Island Ave NW
☎ 333-4372. American. $$

Hunan Chinatown, 113. 624 H St NW
☎ 783-5858. Chinese. $$

I Matti, 5. 2436 18th St NW
☎ 462-8844. Italian. $$

i Ricchi, 55. 1220 19th St NW
☎ 835-0459. Italian. $$$

Il Radicchio, 34. 1509 17th St NW
☎ 986-2627. Italian. $

Iron Gate Inn, 77. 1734 N St NW
☎ 737-1370. Mediterranean. $$

Isabella, 89. 809 15th St NW
☎ 408-9500. Mediterranean. $$

Jaleo, 119. 480 7th St NW
☎ 628-7949. Spanish. $$

Jockey Club, 36.
2100 Massachusetts Ave NW
☎ 659-8000. Continental. $$$$

Kinkead's, 72.
2000 Pennsylvania Ave NW
☎ 296-7700. Seafood. $$$$

La Fourchette, 7. 2429 18th St NW
☎ 332-3077. French. $$

Lauriol Plaza, 22. 1801 18th St NW
☎ 387-0035. Southwestern. $$

Legal Sea Foods, 68. 2020 K St NW
☎ 496-1111. Seafood. $$

Les Halles, 102.
1201 Pennsylvania Ave NW
☎ 347-6848. French. $$$

Lespinasse, 84. 923 16th St NW
☎ 879-6900. French. $$$$

Li Ho Food, 112. 501 H St NW
☎ 289-2059. Szechuan. $$

Luigino, 95. 1100 New York Ave NW
☎ 371-0595. Italian. $$

Luigi's, 63. 1132 19th St NW
☎ 331-7574. Italian. $$

Marrakesh, 107.
617 New York Ave NW
☎ 393-9393. Moroccan. $$

Max's Steakhouse, 75. 1725 F St NW
☎ 842-0070. American. $$$$

Melrose, 46. 2400 M St NW
☎ 955-3899. American. $$$

Mercury Grill, 33. 1602 17th St NW
☎ 667-5937. New American. $$

Meskerem, 8. 2434 18th St NW
☎ 462-4100. Ethiopian. $

Montpelier Room, 87.
15th & M Sts NW
☎ 862-1712. Continental. $$$

Morrison-Clark Inn, 93. 1015 L St NW
☎ 289-8580. American. $$$$

Mr K's, 65. 2121 K St NW
☎ 331-8868. Chinese. $$$$

Mykonos, 70. 1835 K St NW
☎ 331-0370. Greek. $

Nora, 32. 2132 Florida Ave NW
☎ 462-5143. American. $$$

Obelisk, 37. 2029 P St NW
☎ 872-1180. Italian. $$$

Occidental, 98.
1475 Pennsylvania Ave NW
☎ 639-8718. American. $$$

Odeon, 28. 1714 Connecticut Ave NW
☎ 328-6228. Italian. $$

Old Ebbitt Grill, 96. 675 15th St NW
☎ 347-4800. American. $$$

Oodles Noodles, 64. 1010 20th St NW
☎ 293-3138. Asian. $

Palm, 58. 1225 19th St NW
☎ 293-9091. American. $$$$

Pan Asian Noodles & Grill, 37.
2020 P St NW ☎ 872-8889. Thai. $

Peppers, 34. 1527 17th St NW
☎ 328-8193. Southwest. $

Perry's, 2. 1811 Columbia Rd NW
☎ 234-6218. Japanese. $$

MAP **46**

Listed Alphabetically (cont.)

Pesce, 42. 2016 P St NW ☎ 466-3474.
Seafood. $$$

Peyote Café, 12. 2319 18th St NW
☎ 462-8330. Southwestern. $.

Pizza Paradiso, 37. 2029 P St NW
☎ 223-1245. Italian. $$

Planet Hollywood, 104.
1101 Pennsylvania Ave NW
☎ 347-1588. American. $

Polly's Café, 18. 1342 U St NW
☎ 265-8385. American. $$

Prime Rib, 68. 2020 K St NW
☎ 466-8811. American. $$$$

Primi Piatti, 71. 2013 I St NW
☎ 223-3600. Italian. $$

Red Sage, 100. 605 14th St NW
☎ 638-4444. Southwestern. $$$

Red Sea, 6. 2463 18th St NW
☎ 483-5000. Ethiopian. $

Roof Terrace, 52.
Kennedy Center NW
☎ 416-8555. American. $$$

Ruby, 110. 609 H St NW ☎ 842-0060.
Chinese. $

Ruppers, 106. 1017 7th St NW
☎ 783-0699. Contemporary. $$$

Ruth's Chris Steakhouse, 21.
1801 Connecticut Ave NW
☎ 797-0033. Steakhouse. $$$

Saigonnais, 13. 2307 18th St NW
☎ 232-5300. Vietnamese. $$

Sala Thai, 43. 2016 P St NW
☎ 872-1144. Thai. $$

Sam & Harry's, 56. 1200 19th St NW
☎ 296-4333. American. $$$$

701 Pennsylvania, 120.
701 Pennsylvania Ave NW
☎ 393-0701. American. $$$

Skewers, 35. 1633 P St NW
☎ 387-7400. Middle Eastern. $$

Sol, 29. 1739 R St NW ☎ 232-6965.
New Latin. $$

Sostanza, 31. 1606 20th St NW
☎ 667-0047. Italian Steakhouse. $$$

Star of Siam, 61. 1136 19th St NW
☎ 785-2839. Thai. $$

Straits of Malaysia, 20. 1836 18th St
NW ☎ 483-1483. Malaysian. $$-$$$

Tabard Inn, 76. 1739 N St NW
☎ 833-2668. American. $$$

Taberna del Alabardero, 74.
1776 I St NW ☎ 429-2200.
Spanish. $$$$

Teaism, 27. 2009 R St NW
☎ 667-3827. Pan-Asian. $

Tequila Grill, 69. 1990 K St NW
☎ 833-3640. Southwestern. $

Thai Kingdom, 67. 2021 K St NW
☎ 835-1700. Thai. $

Thai Shan, 114. 622 H St NW
☎ 639-0266. Cantonese. $

Tony Cheng's, 109. 619 H St NW
☎ 842-8669. Mongolian. $$

Tuscana West, 91. 1350 I St NW
☎ 289-7300. Italian. $$

Two Continents, 97.
15th & Pennsylvania Ave NW
☎ 347-4499. Continental. $$

Utopia, 16. 1418 U St NW
☎ 483-7669. International. $$-$$$

Vidalia, 57. 1990 M St NW
☎ 659-1990. American. $$$

Washington Grill, 53.
1143 New Hampshire Ave NW
☎ 775-0800. American. $$

West End Cafe, 49.
1 Washington Circle NW
☎ 293-5390. International. $$$

Willard Room, 99.
1401 Pennsylvania Ave NW
☎ 637-7440. American. $$$$

$$$$ = *over $35* $$$ = *$25-$35* $$ = *$15-$25* $ = *under $15*
Based on cost per person, excluding drinks, service, and 9% sales tax.

MAP 47 Dining/Capitol Hill & Waterfront

Listed by Site Number

1	America
1	B. Smith's
1	Pizzeria Uno
2	Capital City Brewing Co
3	Dubliner
4	Irish Times
5	Capitol View Club
6	La Colline
7	Capital Grille
8	Monocle
9	Hunan Capitol Hill
10	American Café
11	La Brasserie
12	White Tiger
13	Armands Pizzeria
14	Two Quail

15	Café Berlin
16	Vie de France Café
17	HI Ribsters
17	Hogate's
18	Le Rivage
19	Philips Flagship
20	Pier 7
21	GangPlank
22	Tortilla Coast
23	Bullfeathers
24	Chesapeake Bagel Bakery
24	Hunan Dynasty
25	Sherrill's Bakery
26	Young Chow
27	Burrito Brothers
28	Hill Cafe

29	Tune Inn
30	Hawk & Dove
31	Market Lunch
32	Mr Henry's
33	Bread & Chocolate
34	Caffé Italiano
35	Cool Breeze's Place
36	Trattoria Alberto

MAP 47

Listed Alphabetically

America, 1. 50 Massachusetts Ave NE
☎ 682–9555. American. $

American Café, 10.
227 Massachusetts Ave NE
☎ 546–7690. American. $

Armands Pizzeria, 13.
226 Massachusetts Ave NE
☎ 547–6600. Italian. $

B. Smith's, 1. 50 Massachusetts Ave
NE ☎ 289–6188. American. $$$

Bread & Chocolate, 33.
666 Pennsylvania Ave SE
☎ 547–2875. French. $

Bullfeathers, 23. 410 1st St SE
☎ 543–5005. American. $

Burrito Brothers, 27.
205 Pennsylvania Ave SE
☎ 543–6835. Mexican. $

Café Berlin, 15.
322 Massachusetts Ave NE
☎ 543–7656. German. $

Caffé Italiano, 34.
1129 Pennsylvania Ave SE
☎ 544–5500. Italian. $

Capital City Brewing Co., 2.
2 Massachusetts Ave NE
☎ 842–2337. American. $$

Capital Grille, 7. 601 Pennsylvania
Ave NW ☎ 737–6200.
Steakhouse. $$$

Capitol View Club, 5.
400 New Jersey Ave NW ☎ 737–1234.
American. $$

Chesapeake Bagel Bakery, 24.
215 Pennsylvania Ave SE
☎ 546–0994. Bakery. $

Cool Breeze's Place, 35. 507 11th St
SE ☎ 543–3184. Chili. $

Dubliner, 3. 520 N Capitol St NW
☎ 737–3773. Irish. $

GangPlank, 21. 600 Water St SW
☎ 554–5000. Seafood. $$

Hawk & Dove, 30.
329 Pennsylvania Ave SE
☎ 543–3300. American. $

HI Ribsters, 17. 800 Water St SW
☎ 479–6857. American. $$

Hill Cafe, 28.
332 Pennsylvania Ave SE
☎ 547–8668. Japanese. $

Hogate's, 17. 800 Water St SW
☎ 484–6301. Seafood. $$$

Hunan Capitol Hill, 9. 201 D St
NE ☎ 544–0102. Chinese. $$

Hunan Dynasty, 24.
215 Pennsylvania Ave SE
☎ 546–6161. Chinese. $

Irish Times, 4. 4 F St NW
☎ 543–5433. Irish. $

La Brasserie, 11.
239 Massachusetts Ave NE
☎ 546–9154. French. $$$

La Colline, 6. 400 N Capitol St NW
☎ 737–0400. French. $$$

Le Rivage, 18. 1000 Water St SW
☎ 488–8111. French. $$

Market Lunch, 31. 225 7th St SE
☎ 547–8444. Seafood. $

Monocle, 8. 107 D St NE
☎ 546–4488. American. $$$

Mr. Henry's, 31. 601 Pennsylvania
Ave SE ☎ 546–8412. American. $

Philips Flagship, 19.
900 Water St SW ☎ 488–8515.
Seafood. $$$

Pier 7, 20. 650 Water St SW
☎ 554–2500. Continental. $$

Pizzeria Uno, 1.
50 Massachusetts Ave NE
☎ 842–0438. American. $$

Sherrill's Bakery, 25.
233 Pennsylvania Ave SE
☎ 544–2480. American. $

Tortilla Coast, 22. 400 1st St SE
☎ 546–6768. Mexican. $$

Trattoria Alberto, 36. 506 8th St SE
☎ 544–2007. Italian. $

Tune Inn, 29. 331½ Pennsylvania
Ave SE ☎ 543–2725. American. $

Two Quail, 14.
320 Massachusetts Ave NE
☎ 543–8030. American/Seafood. $$

Vie de France Café, 16.
600 Maryland Ave SW
☎ 554–7870. French. $

White Tiger, 12. 301 Massachusetts
Ave NE ☎ 546–5900. Thai. $$

Young Chow, 26.
312 Pennsylvania Ave SE
☎ 544–3030. Chinese. $

$$$$ = over $35 $$$ = $25-$35 $$ = $15-$25 $ = under $15
Based on cost per person, excluding drinks, service, and 9% sales tax.

MAP 48 Dining/Georgetown

Listed by Site Number

MAP **48**

Listed Alphabetically

Aditi, 11. 3299 M St NW ☎ 625-6825. Indian. $$

Au Pied du Cochon, 3. 1335 Wisconsin Ave NW ☎ 333-5440. French. $

Bistro Français, 19. 3128 M St NW ☎ 338-3830. French. $$$

Burrito Brothers, 18. 3273 M St NW ☎ 965-3963. Mexican. $

Café La Ruche, 39. 1039 31st St NW ☎ 965-2684. French. $

Café Milano, 5. 3251 Prospect St NW ☎ 333-6183. Italian. $$

Chadwick's Georgetown, 37. 3205 K St NW ☎ 333-2565. American. $

Charing Cross, 27. 3027 M St NW ☎ 338-2141. Italian. $

Citronelle, 25. 3000 M St NW (Latham Hotel) ☎ 625-2150. American. $$$

Clyde's, 13. 3236 M St NW ☎ 333-9180. American. $$

El Caribe, 12. 3288 M St NW ☎ 338-3121. Latin American. $$$

Enriqueta's, 28. 2811 M St NW ☎ 338-7772. Mexican. $$

Fettoosh, 14. 3277 M St NW ☎ 342-1199. Lebanese. $

Filomena's, 34. 1063 Wisconsin Ave NW ☎ 338-8800. Italian. $$

Garretts, 23. 3003 M St NW ☎ 333-1033. American. $

Georgetown Seafood, 21. 3063 M St NW ☎ 333-7038. Seafood. $$

Gepettos, 24. 2917 M St NW ☎ 333-2602. Italian. $

The Guards, 24. 2915 M St NW ☎ 965-2350. American. $$

Hibiscus Café, 32. 3401 K St NW ☎ 965-7170. Caribbean. $$

Houston's, 33. 1065 Wisconsin Ave NW ☎ 338-7760. American. $$

Il Radicchio, 8. 1211 Wisconsin Ave NW ☎ 337-2627. Italian. $$

Japan Inn, 1. 1715 Wisconsin Ave NW ☎ 337-3400. Japanese. $$

La Chaumière, 27. 2813 M St NW ☎ 338-1784. French. $$$

Martin's Tavern, 6. 1264 Wisconsin Ave NW ☎ 333-7370. American. $

Morton's of Chicago, 5. 3251 Prospect St NW ☎ 342-6258. Steakhouse. $$$$

Mr. Smith's, 20. 3104 M St NW ☎ 333-3104. American. $$

Music City Roadhouse, 36. 1050 30th St NW ☎ 337-4444. Southern. $

Nathan's, 17. 3150 M St NW ☎ 338-2000. Italian. $$$

Paolo's, 20. 1303 Wisconsin Ave NW ☎ 333-7353. Italian. $$

Paper Moon, 38. 1069 31st St NW ☎ 965-6666. Italian. $$

Pizzeria Uno, 16. 3211 M St NW ☎ 965-6333. American. $

Provence, 30. 2401 Pennsylvania Ave NW ☎ 296-1166. French. $$$

Samurai by Benihana, 15. 3222 M St NW ☎ 333-1001. Japanese. $$

Sea Catch, 35. 1054 31 St NW ☎ 337-8855. Seafood. $$$

Seasons, 31. 2800 Pennsylvania Ave NW (Four Seasons Hotel) ☎ 342-0810. Continental. $$$$

Sequoia, 40. 3000 K St NW ☎ 944-4920. American. $$

1789, 4. 1226 36th St NW ☎ 965-1789. American. $$$$

Tandoor, 10. 3316 M St NW ☎ 333-3376. Indian. $

Third Edition, 7. 1218 Wisconsin Ave NW ☎ 333-3700. American. $

The Tombs, 4. 1226 36th St NW ☎ 337-6668. American. $

Tony & Joe's, 41. 3000 K St NW ☎ 944-4545. Seafood. $$$

Vietnam Georgetown, 26. 2934 M St NW ☎ 337-4536. Vietnamese. $

Vintage, 29. 2809 M St NW ☎ 625-0077. French. $$$

Zed's Ethiopian Cuisine, 9. 3318 M St NW ☎ 333-4710. Ethiopian. $

$$$$ = over $35 $$$ = $25-$35 $$ = $15-$25 $ = under $15
Based on cost per person, excluding drinks, service, and 9% sales tax.

MAP 49 Dining/Northwest

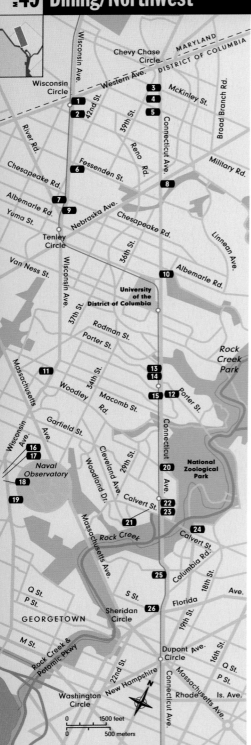

MAP 49

Listed Alphabetically

American City Diner, 4.
5532 Connecticut Ave NW
☎ 244-1949. American. $

Austin Grill, 17. 2404 Wisconsin Ave NW
☎ 337-8080. Tex-Mex. $

Bread & Chocolate, 3.
5542 Connecticut Ave NW
☎ 966-7413. French. $

Cactus Cantina, 11.
3300 Wisconsin Ave NW
☎ 686-7222. Tex-Mex. $$

Caffe Italiano, 14.
3615 Connecticut Ave NW
☎ 966-2172. Italian. $$

Calvert Restaurant, 24.
1967 Calvert St NW
☎ 232-5431. Middle Eastern. $

Chadwick's, 2. 5247 Wisconsin Ave NW
☎ 362-8040. American. $$

Cheesecake Factory, 1.
5335 Wisconsin Ave NW
☎ 364-0500. American. $$

Dancing Crab, 9.
4611 Wisconsin Ave NW
☎ 244-1882. Seafood. $$

Germaine's, 18.
2400 Wisconsin Ave NW
☎ 965-1185. Asian. $$

Ireland's Four Provinces, 15.
3412 Connecticut Ave NW
☎ 244-0860. Irish. $$

Ivy's Place, 13.
3520 Connecticut Ave NW
☎ 363-7802. Thai. $

Krupins Deli, 9. 4620 Wisconsin Ave
NW ☎ 686-1989. American. $$

Lavandou, 12.
3321 Connecticut Ave NW
☎ 966-3002. French. $$

Lebanese Taverna, 22.
2641 Connecticut Ave NW
☎ 265-8681. Middle Eastern. $$

Mrs. Simpson's, 20.
2915 Connecticut Ave NW
☎ 332-8300. American. $$

New Heights, 21. 2317 Calvert St NW
☎ 234-4110. American. $$$

Old Europe, 16.
2434 Wisconsin Ave NW
☎ 333-7600. German. $$

Parthenon, 5.
5510 Connecticut Ave NW
☎ 966-7600. Greek. $$

Round Table, 6.
4859 Wisconsin Ave NW
☎ 362-1250. Italian/American. $$

Russia House, 26.
1800 Connecticut Ave NW
☎ 986-6010. Russian. $$

Shanghai Garden, 10.
4469 Connecticut Ave NW
☎ 362-3000. Chinese. $

Sushi-Ko. 19. 2309 Wisconsin
Ave NW ☎ 333-4187.
Japanese. $$

Thai Room, 8.
5037 Connecticut Ave NW
☎ 244-5933. Thai. $

Thai Town, 27. 2655 Connecticut Ave
NW ☎ 667-5115. Asian. $$

Trocadero Café, 25.
1914 Connecticut Ave NW
☎ 797-2000. French. $$$

Yosaku, 7. 4712 Wisconsin Ave NW
☎ 363-4453. Japanese. $$

$$$$ = *over $35* $$$ = *$25-$35* $$ = *$15-$25* $ = *under $15*
Based on cost per person, excluding drinks, service, and 9% sales tax.

MAP 50 Mall Lunch Spots

George Washington University

World Bank

Old Executive Office Bldg.

White House

General Services Bldg.

Dept. of State

Freedom Plaza

The Ellipse

Commerce Dept.

National Museum of American History

Washington Convention Center

Explorers Hall

Bus Terminal

Thomas Circle

Vietnam Veterans Memorial

Reflecting Pool

Lincoln Memorial

Korean War Veterans Memorial

Washington Monument

THE MALL

Smithsonian Institution

Jefferson Dr.

Independence

Tidal Basin

West Potomac Park

Potomac River

FDR Memorial

Jefferson Memorial

Outlet Br.

Listed Alphabetically

Air & Space Museum Cafeteria, 32.
Independence Ave & 6th St SW

American History Museum Cafeteria, 29. Madison Dr & 13th St NW

Au Bon Pain, 10. 1401 I St NW

Bertucci's, 1.
2000 Pennsylvania Ave NW

Bread Line, 3.
1751 Pennsylvania Ave NW

Cafe Mozart, 12. 1331 H St NW

Corcoran Gallery, 6. 500 17th St NW

Department of Agriculture, 33.
Independence Ave & 13th St SW

Department of Health & Human Services, 36.
330 Independence Ave SW

Department of Housing & Urban Development, 35. 451 7th St SW

Department of the Interior, 7.
1800 C St NW

Dirksen Senate Office Cafeteria, 39. Constitution Ave & First St NE

Dutch Mill Deli, 26.
639 Indiana Ave NW

Federal Trade Commission, 27.
Pennsylvania Ave & 6th St NW

Friday's, 19.
1201 Pennsylvania Ave NW

Gourmet Too, 34.
609 L'Enfant Plaza East SW

Hard Rock Cafe, 23. 999 E St NW

Hirshhorn Outdoor Cafe, 31.
Independence Ave & 7th St SW

Hot Shoppes, 5.
1750 Pennsylvania Ave NW

Hotel Washington, 15.
515 15th St NW

International Sq, 2. 1850 K St NW

International Trade Center, 17.
E and 14th Sts NW

MAP 50

MAP 51 Dining/Metropolitan Area

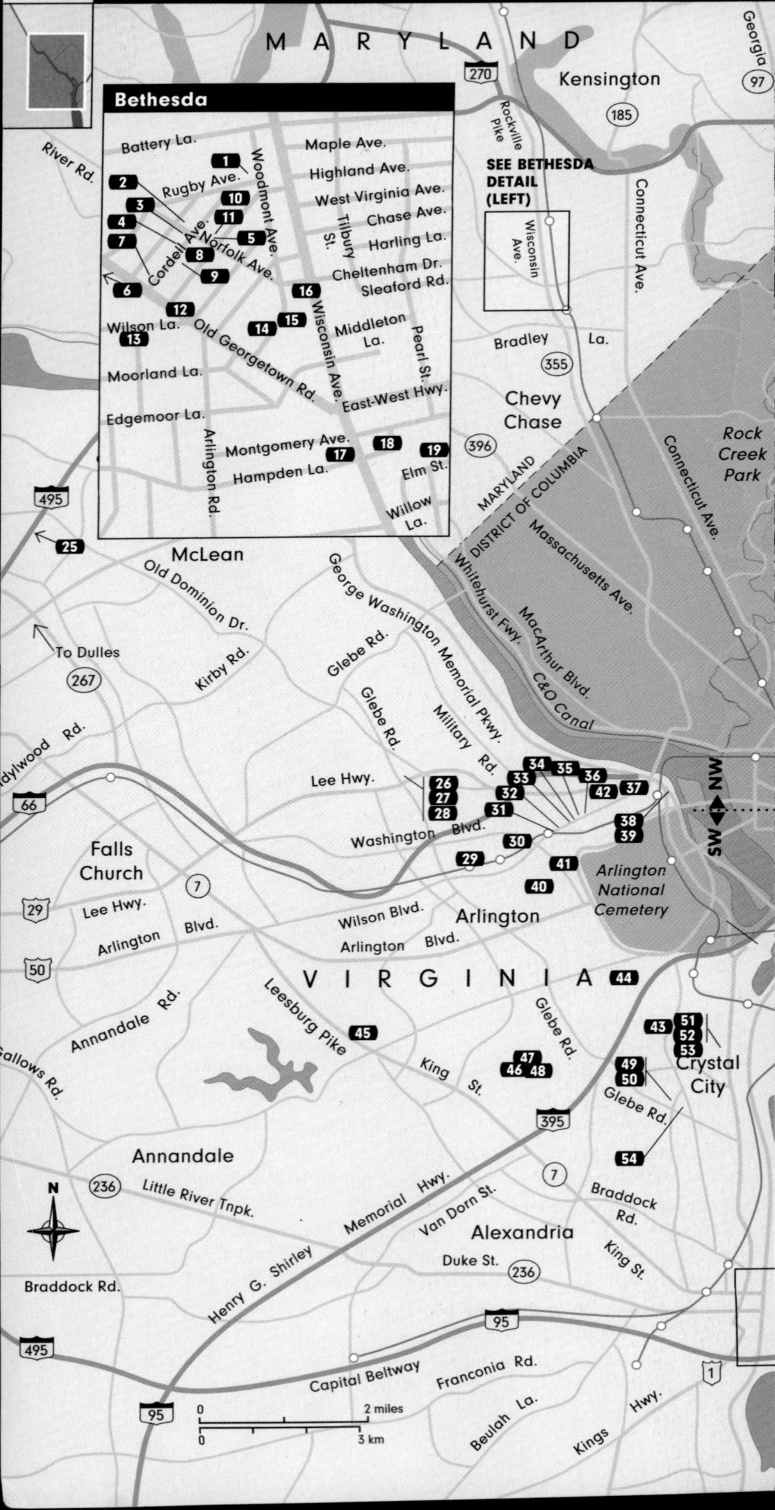

MARYLAND

Kensington

270

97

185

Rockville Pike

SEE BETHESDA
DETAIL
(LEFT)

Connecticut Ave.

Wisconsin Ave.

355

Bethesda

Battery La.

Maple Ave.

Highland Ave.

West Virginia Ave.

Rugby Ave.

1

2

10

Chase Ave.

3

11

Tilbury St.

Harling La.

4

5

7

Woodmont Ave.

8

Cordell Ave.

Norfolk Ave.

9

Cheltenham Dr.

Sleaford Rd.

6

16

Middleton La.

12

14

15

Wisconsin Ave.

Wilson La.

13

Old Georgetown Rd.

Pearl St.

Moorland La.

East-West Hwy.

Edgemoor La.

Arlington Rd.

Montgomery Ave.

17

18

19

Hampden La.

Elm St.

Willow La.

396

Bradley La.

Chevy Chase

MARYLAND

DISTRICT OF COLUMBIA

Massachusetts Ave.

Rock Creek Park

Connecticut Ave.

River Rd.

McLean

Old Dominion Dr.

To Dulles

267

Kirby Rd.

George Washington Memorial Pkwy.

Whitehurst Fwy.

MacArthur Blvd.

C&O Canal

Idylwood Rd.

Glebe Rd.

Glebe Rd.

Military Rd.

NW

SW

NE

SE

495

25

66

Lee Hwy.

26

27

28

33

34

35

36

42

37

32

31

38

39

Washington Blvd.

30

29

41

40

Arlington National Cemetery

Falls Church

29

Lee Hwy.

7

Arlington Blvd.

Wilson Blvd.

Arlington Blvd.

Arlington

50

VIRGINIA

44

Annandale Rd.

Leesburg Pike

45

King St.

Glebe Rd.

43

51
52
53

47
46 48

49
50

Crystal City

Glebe Rd.

Gallows Rd.

395

54

Braddock Rd.

Annandale

236

Little River Tnpk.

N

Henry G. Shirley Memorial Hwy.

Van Dorn St.

Alexandria

Duke St.

236

King St.

Braddock Rd.

495

95

95

Capital Beltway

Franconia Rd.

Beulah La.

Kings Hwy.

1

0   2 miles
0   3 km

Georgia

Woodmont Ave.

Listed by Site Number

Listed Alphabetically

BETHESDA, MD

Andalucia 19. 4931 Elm St
☎ 301/907-0052. Spanish. $$$

Bacchus-Bethesda, 2. 7945 Norfolk Ave
☎ 301/657-1722. Lebanese. $$

Cafe Bethesda, 13. 5027 Wilson Lane
☎ 301/657-3383. American. $$

Calasia, 4. 7929 Norfolk Ave
☎ 301/654-6444. Asian-American. $$$

Cottonwood Café, 8. 4844 Cordell Ave
☎ 301/656-4844. American. $$

Frascati, 1. 4806 Rugby Ave
☎ 301/652-9514. Italian. $$

Haandi, 15. 4904 Fairmont Ave
☎ 301/718-0121. Indian. $

Jean-Michel, 6. 10223 Old G'town Rd
☎ 301/564-4910. French. $$

La Madelaine, 12. 7607 Old G'town
Rd ☎ 301/215-9139. Bakery/Cafe. $

La Miche, 11. 7905 Norfolk Ave
☎ 301/986-0707. French. $$$

La Panetteria, 4. 4921 Cordell Ave
☎ 301/951-6433. Italian. $$

Matuba, 9. 4918 Cordell Ave
☎ 301/652-7449. Japanese. $$

North China, 7. 7814 Old Georgetown
Rd ☎ 301/656-7922. Chinese. $

Pines of Rome, 17. 4709 Hampden La
☎ 301/657-8775. Italian. $

Rio Grande, 14. 4919 Fairmont Ave
☎ 301/656-2981. Tex-Mex. $

Tako Grill, 16. 7756 Wisconsin Ave
☎ 301/652-7030. Japanese. $$

Tastee Diner, 10. 7731 Woodmont
Ave ☎ 301/652-3970. American. $

Tragara, 3. 4935 Cordell Ave
☎ 301/951-9935. Italian. $$$

Vagabond, 18. 7315 Wisconsin Ave
☎ 301/654-2575. Romanian. $$

SILVER SPRING, MD

Crisfield, 24. 8012 Georgia Ave
☎ 301/589-1306. Seafood. $$

Fred & Harry's, 20. 10110 Colesville Rd
☎ 301/593-7177. Seafood. $$

Golden Flame, 21. 8630 Fenton St
☎ 301/588-7250. Continental. $$

Mrs K's Tollhouse, 22. 9201 Colesville
Rd ☎ 301/589-3500. American. $$

Siddhartha, 23. 8241 Georgia Ave
☎ 301/585-0550. Indian/Vegetarian. $

GREAT FALLS, VA

L'Auberge Chez Francois, 26. 332 Spring-
vale Rd ☎ 703/759-3800. French. $$$$

ARLINGTON, VA

Alpine, 27. 4770 Lee Hwy
☎ 703/528-7600. Italian. $$

Bistro Bistro, 44. 4021 S. 28th St
☎ 703/379-0300. American. $$

Blue & Gold, 41. 3100 Clarendon Blvd
☎ 703/908-4995. Brewpub. $$

Bob & Edith's, 44. 2310 Columbia
Pike ☎ 703/920-6103. Diner. $

Cafe Dalat, 34. 3143 Wilson Blvd
☎ 703/276-0935. Vietnamese. $

Carlyle Grand, 47. 4000 S. 28th St
☎ 703/931-0777. American. $$

**Chesapeake Seafood Crab
House, 40.** 3607 Wilson Blvd
☎ 703/528-8888. Vietnamese. $

Duangrat's, 45. 5878 Leesburg Pike
☎ 703/820-5775. Thai. $$

Faccia Luna, 42. 2909 Wilson Blvd
☎ 703/276-3099. Italian. $$

L'Alouette, 38. 2045 Wilson Blvd
☎ 703/525-1750. French. $$

Little Viet Garden, 33. 3012 Wilson
Blvd ☎ 703/522-9686. Vietnamese. $

Orleans House, 39. 1213 Wilson Blvd
☎ 703/524-2929. American. $$

Pasha Café, 28. 3815 Lee Hwy
☎ 703/528-2126. Egyptian. $$

Pho 75, 32. 1711 Wilson Blvd
☎ 703/525-7355. Vietnamese. $

Pines of Capri, 30. 2721 N Washington Blvd ☎ 703/276-8789. Italian. $

Pizzeria Uno, 36. 4201 Wilson Blvd
☎ 703/527-8988. Italian. $

Portofino, 50. 526 S 23rd St
☎ 703/979-8200. Italian. $$

Queen Bee, 35. 3181 Wilson Blvd
☎ 703/527-3444. Vietnamese. $

Red, Hot & Blue, 31. 1600 Wilson Blvd
☎ 703/276-7427. Southern/BBQ. $

Rio Grande, 29. 4301 N Fairfax Dr
☎ 703/528-3131. Tex-Mex. $

Shanghai, 27. 5157 Lee Hwy
☎ 703/536-7446. Chinese. $

Thai in Shirlington, 46. 4029 S. 28th
St ☎ 703/931-3203. Thai. $$

The View, 37. 1401 Lee Hwy
☎ 703/243-1745. American. $$$

Pendleton St.

Oronoco St.

Princess St.

Queen St. **67** **68**

Cameron St. **70**
66 **69** **71**

King St. **72**
64 **65** **73**
64 **74**

Prince St.

75

Wolfe St.

N. West St.
N. Payne St.
N. Fayette St.
N. Henry St.
N. Patrick St.
N. Alfred St.
N. Columbus St.
N. Washington St.
N. Fairfax St.
N. Lee St.
N. Union St.

59 **60**

King St.
57
58 **62**
61 **63**

Prince St.
56
Duke St.

S. Patrick St.
S. Alfred St.
S. Columbus St.
S. Washington St.
S. St. Asaph St.
S. Pitt St.
S. Royal St.
S. Fairfax St.
S. Lee St.
S. Union St.

Potomac River

N

0 ____ 1200 feet
0 ____ 400 meters

Listed Alphabetically (cont.)

Whitlow's on Wilson, 33. 2854 Wilson Blvd ☎ 703/525-9825. Diner. $

CRYSTAL CITY, VA
Bangkok Gourmet, 51. 523 S 23rd St ☎ 703/521-1305. Thai. $$

Chez Froggy, 52. 509 S 23rd St ☎ 703/979-7676. French. $$$

Endoya, 43. 2301 S. Jefferson Davis Hwy ☎ 703/418-2344. Japanese. $$

ALEXANDRIA, VA
Alamo, 73. 1100 King St ☎ 703/739-0555. Mexican. $$

Bilbo Baggins, 67. 208 Queen St ☎ 703/683-0300. American. $$

California Pizza Kitchen, 62. 700 King St ☎ 703/706-0404. Italian. $

Chadwick's, 75. 203 S. Strand St ☎ 703/836-4442. American. $$

Chart House, 70. 1 Cameron St ☎ 703/684-5080. American. $$$

Chez André, 49. 10 E Glebe Rd ☎ 703/836-1404. French. $$

East Wind, 59. 809 King St ☎ 703/836-1515. Vietnamese. $$

Fish Market, 72. 105 King St ☎ 703/836-5676. Seafood. $$

Gadsby's Tavern, 66. 138 N Royal St ☎ 703/548-1288. American. $$$

Geranio, 61. 722 King St ☎ 703/548-0088. Italian. $$

Il Porto, 69. 121 King St ☎ 703/836-8833. Italian. $$

La Bergerie, 68. 218 N Lee St ☎ 703/683-1007. French. $$$

Le Gaulois, 57. 1106 King St ☎ 703/739-9494. French. $$

La Madelaine, 64. 500 King St ☎ 703/739-2853. Bakery/Cafe. $

Le Refuge, 63. 127 N Washington St ☎ 703/548-4661. French. $$$

Potowmack Landing, 55. Washington Marina ☎ 703/548-0001. Seafood. $$$

R T's, 54. 3804 Mt Vernon St ☎ 703/684-6010. Seafood. $$

Santa Fe East, 65. 110 Pitt St ☎ 703/548-6900. Mexican. $$

South Austin Grill, 60. 801 King St ☎ 703/684-8969. Tex-Mex. $

Taverna Cretekou, 58. 818 King St ☎ 703/548-8688. Greek. $$$

Union St Public Hse, 71. 121 S Union St ☎ 703/548-1785. American. $$

The Wharf, 74. 119 King St ☎ 703/836-2834. Seafood. $$$

Woo Lae Oak, 53. 1500 S. Joyce St ☎ 703/521-3706. Korean. $

$$$$ = *over $35* $$$ = *$25-$35* $$ = *$15-$25* $ = *under $15*
Based on cost per person, excluding drinks, service, and 9% sales tax in DC, 4.5% in VA, and 5% in MD

MAP 52 Lodging/Downtown

Listed by Site Number

1 Holiday Inn-Georgetown
2 Savoy Suites
3 Days Inn-Uptown
4 Kalorama-Woodley
5 Omni Shoreham
6 Marriott Wardman-Park
7 Kalorama-Kalorama Park
8 Adams Inn
9 Hotel Windsor Park
10 Normandy Inn
11 Sofitel
12 Washington Courtyard
13 Washington Hilton
14 Carlyle Suites
15 Windsor Inn
16 Embassy Inn
17 Embassy Row
18 Radisson Barcelo
19 ITT-Luxury Collection
20 Georgetown Inn
21 Latham
22 Four Seasons
23 Doubletree Guest Suites
24 Wyndham Bristol
25 River Inn
26 Inn at Foggy Bottom
27 Watergate
28 Howard Johnson's
29 Doubletree Guest Suites
30 Lombardy
31 One Washington Cir
32 The Westin
33 Park Hyatt
34 ANA Hotel
35 Embassy Suites
36 Washington Marriott
37 Sheraton City Center
38 Lincoln Suites
39 Embassy Square Suites
40 Hampshire
41 Tabard Inn
42 Canterbury
43 Governors House

MAP 52

Listed by Site Number (cont.)

Listed Alphabetically

Adams Inn, 8. 1744 Lanier Pl NW
☎ 745-3600. $

ANA Hotel, 34. 2401 M St NW
☎ 429-2400. 📠 457-5010. $$$$

AYH Hostel, 58. 1009 11th St NW
☎ 737-2333. $

Bellevue, 75. 15 E St NW
☎ 638-0900. 📠 638-5132. $$

Best Western Skyline Inn, 82. 10 I St SW
☎ 488-7500. 📠 488-0790. $

Canterbury, 42. 1733 N St NW
☎ 393-3000. 📠 785-9581. $$$

Capital Hilton, 61. 1001 16th St NW
☎ 393-1000. 📠 639-5784. $$$$

Capitol Hill Suites, 79. 200 C St SE
☎ 543-6000. 📠 547-2608. $$$

Carlton, 62. 923 16th St NW
☎ 638-2626. 📠 638-4231. $$$$

Carlyle Suites, 14. 1731 New
Hampshire Ave NW ☎ 234-3200.
📠 387-0085. $

Center City Travel Lodge, 55.
1201 13th St NW ☎ 682-5300.
📠 371-9624. $

Channel Inn, 80. 650 Water St SW
☎ 554-2400. 📠 863-1164. $$

Comfort Inn, 71. 500 H St NW
☎ 289-5959. 📠 682-9152. $

Crowne Plaza, 54. 1001 14th St NW
☎ 682-0111. 📠 682-9525. $$$

Days Inn-Convention Center, 57.
1201 K St NW ☎ 842-1020.
📠 289-0336. $

Days Inn-Uptown, 3.
4400 Connecticut Ave NW
☎ 244-5600. 📠 244-6794. $

Doubletree Guest Suites, 23.
2500 Pennsylvania Ave NW
☎ 333-8060. 📠 338-3818. $$$

Doubletree Guest Suites, 29.
801 New Hampshire Ave NW
☎ 785-2000. 📠 785-9485. $$$

Doubletree Park Terrace, 45.
1515 Rhode Island Ave NW
☎ 232-7000. 📠 332-7152. $$$

Embassy Inn, 16. 1627 16th St NW
☎ 234-7800. 📠 234-3309. $

Embassy Row, 17. 2015 Mass Ave
NW ☎ 265-1600. 📠 328-7526. $$$

Embassy Square Suites, 39.
2000 N St NW
☎ 659-9000. 📠 429-9546. $$

Embassy Suites, 35. 1250 22nd St NW
☎ 857-3388. 📠 293-3173. $$$

Four Seasons, 22. 2800 Penn Ave
NW ☎ 342-0444. 📠 944-2076. $$$$

Georgetown Inn, 20.
1310 Wisconsin Ave NW
☎ 333-8900. 📠 625-1744. $$$

Governors House, 43. 1615 Rhode
Island Ave NW ☎ 296-2100.
📠 331-0227. $

Grand Hyatt, 69. 1000 H St NW
☎ 582-1234. 📠 637-4781. $$$$

Hampshire, 40.
1310 New Hampshire Ave NW
☎ 296-7600. 📠 293-2476. $$

Harrington, 67. 436 11th St NW
☎ 628-8140. 📠 393-2311. $

Hay-Adams, 63. 800 16th St NW
☎ 638-6600. 📠 638-2716. $$$$

Henley Park, 59.
926 Massachusetts Ave NW
☎ 638-5200. 📠 638-6740. $$$

Holiday Inn-Capitol, 77.
415 New Jersey Ave NW
☎ 638-1616. 📠 638-0707. $$

Holiday Inn-Capitol, 78. 550 C St SW
☎ 479-4000. 📠 479-4353. $$

Holiday Inn-Central, 46.
1501 Rhode Island Ave NW
☎ 483-2000. 📠 797-1078. $

Holiday Inn-Franklin Square, 53.
1155 14th St NW ☎ 737-1200.
📠 783-5733. $$

Holiday Inn-Georgetown, 1.
2101 Wisconsin Ave NW
☎ 338-4600. 📠 333-6113. $$

Hotel Washington, 64. 515 15th St NW
☎ 638-5900. 📠 638-4275. $$

Hotel Windsor Park, 9.
2116 Kalorama Rd NW
☎ 483-7700. 📠 332-4547. $

Howard Johnson, 47.
1430 Rhode Island Ave NW
☎ 462-7777. 📠 332-3519. $

Howard Johnson Inn, 60.
600 New York Ave NE
☎ 546-9200. 📠 546-6348. $

Howard Johnson's, 28.
2601 Virginia Ave NW
☎ 965-2700. 📠 337-5417. $

Hyatt Regency, 76.
400 New Jersey Ave NW
☎ 737-1234. 📠 393-7927. $$$$

Inn at Foggy Bottom, 26.
824 New Hampshire Ave NW
☎ 337-6620. 📠 298-7499. $$

MAP 52

Listed Alphabetically (cont.)

ITT-Luxury Collection, 19.
2100 Massachusetts Ave NW
☎ 293-2100. 📠 736-1420. $$$$

Jefferson, 48. 1200 16th St NW
☎ 347-2200. 📠 331-7982. $$$$

JW Marriott, 66. 1331 Penn Ave NW
☎ 393-2000. 📠 626-6991. $$$$

Kalorama Guesthouse at Kalorama Park, 7. 1854 Mintwood Pl NW
☎ 667-6369. $

Kalorama Guesthouse at Woodley Park, 4. 2700 Cathedral Ave NW
☎ 328-0860. $

Latham, 21. 3000 M St NW
☎ 726-5000. 📠 337-4250. $$$

Lincoln Suites, 38. 1823 L St NW
☎ 223-4320. 📠 223-8546. $$$

Loew's L'Enfant Plaza, 81.
480 L'Enfant Plaza SW
☎ 484-1000. 📠 646-4456. $$$

Lombardy, 30.
2019 Pennsylvania Ave NW
☎ 828-2600. 📠 872-0503. $$

Madison, 50. 1177 15th St NW
☎ 862-1600. 📠 785-1255. $$$$

Marriot Metro Center, 68.
775 12th St NW ☎ 737-2200.
📠 347-5886. $$$

Marriott Wardman-Park, 6.
2660 Woodley Rd NW
☎ 328-2000. 📠 234-0015. $$$

Mayflower, 49. 1127 Connecticut Ave NW
☎ 347-3000. 📠 776-9182. $$$$

Morrison-Clark Inn, 56. 1015 L St NW
☎ 898-1200. 📠 289-8576. $$$

Normandy Inn, 10. 2118 Wyoming Ave NW ☎ 483-1350. 📠 387-8241. $

Omni Shoreham, 5. 2500 Calvert St NW
☎ 234-0700. 📠 232-4140. $$$$

One Washington Circle, 31.
1 Washington Circle NW
☎ 872-1680. 📠 887-4989. $$$

Park Hyatt, 32. 1201 24th St NW
☎ 789-1234. 📠 457-8823. $$$$

Phoenix Park, 74. 520 N Capitol St NW
☎ 638-6900. 📠 393-3236. $$$

Quality Hotel-Downtown, 44.
1315 16th St NW
☎ 232-8000. 📠 667-9827. $

Radisson Barcelo, 18. 2121 P St NW ☎ 293-3100. 📠 857-0134. $$$

River Inn, 25. 924 25th St NW
☎ 337-7600. 📠 337-6520. $$$

Savoy Suites, 2. 2505 Wisconsin Ave NW
☎ 337-9700. 📠 337-3644. $$

Sheraton City Centre, 37.
1143 New Hampshire Ave NW
☎ 775-0800. 📠 331-9491. $$$

Sofitel, 11. 1914 Connecticut Ave NW
☎ 797-2000. 📠 462-0944. $$$

Super 8 Washington, 72.
501 New York Ave NE
☎ 543-7400. 📠 544-2327. $

Tabard Inn, 41. 1739 N St NW
☎ 785-1277. 📠 785-6173. $$

Washington Court, 73.
525 New Jersey Ave NW
☎ 628-2100. 📠 879-7918. $$$$

Washington Courtyard, 12. 1900 Connecticut Ave NW ☎ 332-9300.
📠 328-7039. $$

Washington DC Renaissance at Tech World, 70. 999 9th St NW
☎ 898-9000. 📠 289-0947. $$$

Washington Hilton, 13.
1919 Connecticut Ave NW
☎ 483-3000. 📠 232-0438. $$$$

Washington Marriott, 36. 1221 22nd St NW ☎ 872-1500. 📠 872-1424. $$$$

Washington Plaza, 52. 10 Thomas Cir NW ☎ 842-1300. 📠 371-9602. $$$

Washington Vista, 51. 1400 M St NW
☎ 429-1700. 📠 785-0786. $$$

Watergate, 27. 2650 Virginia Ave NW
☎ 965-2300. 📠 337-7915. $$$$

The Westin Hotel, 32. 2350 M St NW
☎ 429-0100. 📠 429-9759. $$$

Willard Inter-Continental, 65.
1401 Pennsylvania Ave NW
☎ 628-9100. 📠 637-7326. $$$$

Windsor Inn, 15. 1842 16th St NW
☎ 667-0300. 📠 667-4503. $

Wyndham Bristol, 24.
2430 Pennsylvania Ave NW
☎ 955-6400. 📠 955-5765. $$$

$$$$ = over $190 $$$ = $130-$190 $$ = $100-$130 $ = under $100
All prices are for a standard double room, excluding 10% room tax, and are weekday rates; weekend rates are often reduced.

MAP 53 Lodging/Metropolitan Area

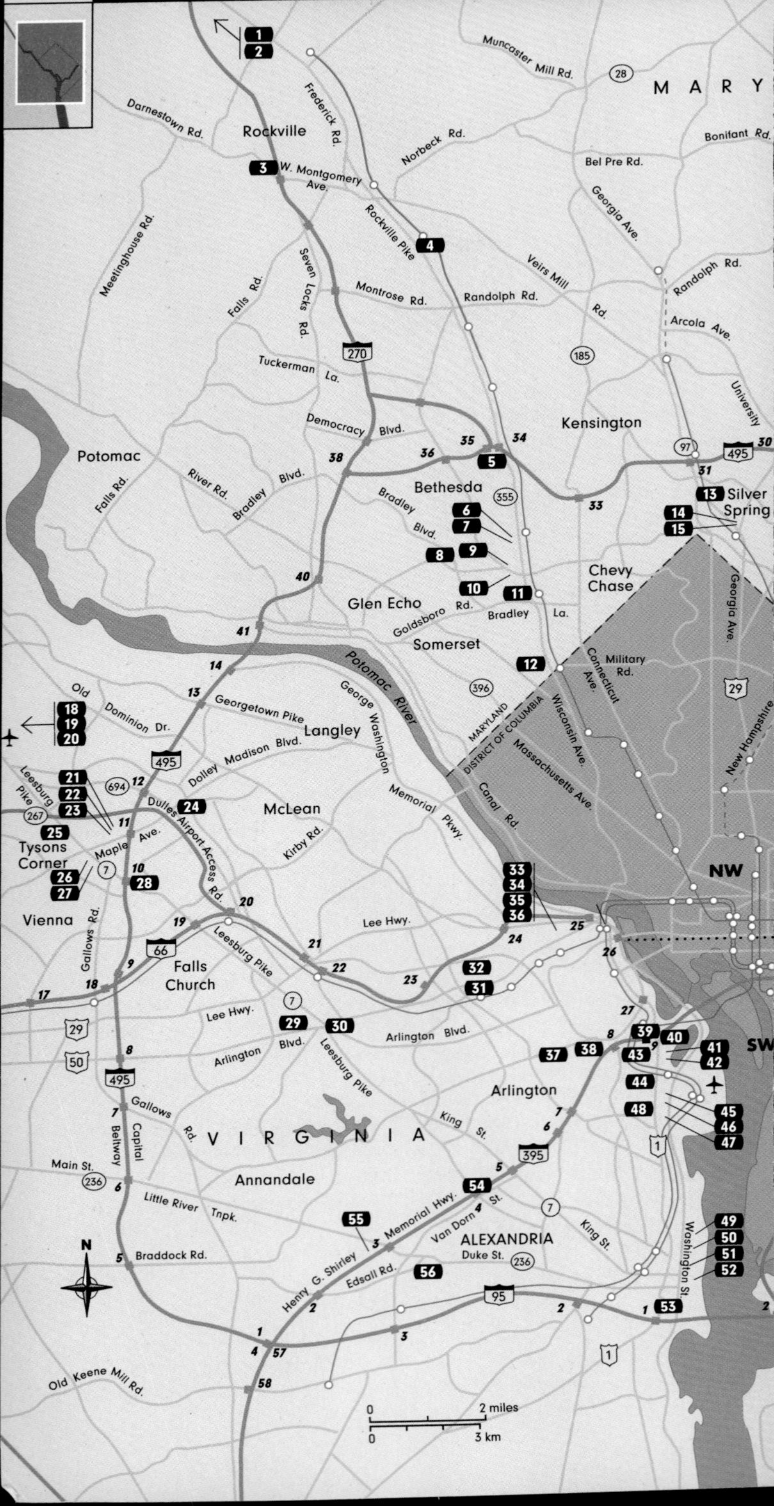

MARYLAND

Muncaster Mill Rd.
28
Bonifant Rd.
Bel Pre Rd.
Georgia Ave.
Darnestown Rd.
Rockville
3 W. Montgomery Ave.
Frederick Rd.
Norbeck Rd.
Randolph Rd.
Veirs Mill Rd.
Arcola Ave.
University
Meetinghouse Rd.
Falls Rd.
Seven Locks Rd.
Rockville Pike
4
Montrose Rd.
Randolph Rd.
185
270
Tuckerman La.
Democracy Blvd.
Kensington
97
495 30
31
Potomac
River Rd.
Bradley Blvd.
Falls Rd.
38
36
35 34
5
Bethesda
355
33
13 Silver Spring
14
15
Bradley Blvd.
6
7
8 9
40
10
11
Glen Echo
Goldsboro Rd.
Bradley La.
Chevy Chase
Military Rd.
Somerset
41
14
Potomac River
396
12
Connecticut Ave.
Wisconsin Ave.
29
13
Georgetown Pike
Langley
MARYLAND
DISTRICT OF COLUMBIA
Massachusetts Ave.
New Hampshire
Old Dominion Dr.
18
19
20
George Washington Memorial Pkwy.
Dolley Madison Blvd.
Leesburg Pike
267
21
22
23
694
12
Dulles Airport Access Rd.
24
McLean
Kirby Rd.
NW
25
11
Maple Ave.
7
10
28
Tysons Corner
26
27
Vienna
Gallows Rd.
9
66
19
Leesburg Pike
20
Lee Hwy.
33
34
35
36
24
25
26
Falls Church
17
18
8
21
22
23
32
31
27
29
50
495
29 30
Arlington Blvd.
Leesburg Pike
37 38
8
39 40
43
41
42
SW
Lee Hwy.
Arlington Blvd.
Arlington
44
48
45
46
47
VIRGINIA
7
Capital Beltway
Gallows Rd.
King St.
6
236
6
Main St.
Little River Tnpk.
Annandale
5
395
54
1
5
Braddock Rd.
Henry G. Shirley Memorial Hwy.
55
3
Memorial Hwy.
Van Dorn St.
ALEXANDRIA
Duke St.
236
King St.
Washington St.
49
50
51
52
Edsall Rd.
56
2
95
2
1
53
Old Keene Mill Rd.
4
57
1
3
1
58

N

0 2 miles
0 3 km

MAP
53

Listed Alphabetically

BETHESDA, MD

American Inn, 8.
8130 Wisconsin Ave
☎ 301/656-9300. 🖷 656-2907. $

Bethesda Court Hotel, 10. 7740
Wisconsin Ave ☎ 301/656-2100.
🖷 986-0375. $

Holiday Inn, 7. 8120 Wisconsin Ave
☎ 301/652-2000. 🖷 652-4525. $$

Hyatt Regency, 9. 7400 Wisconsin Ave
☎ 301/657-1234. 🖷 657-6453. $$

Marriott, 5. 5151 Pooks Hill Rd
☎ 301/897-9400. 🖷 897-0192. $$$

Ramada Inn, 6. 8400 Wisconsin Ave
☎ 301/654-1000. 🖷 654-0751. $$

Residence Inn, 11.
7335 Wisconsin Ave
☎ 301/718-0200. 🖷 718-0679. $$$

CHEVY CHASE, MD

Holiday Inn, 12. 5520 Wisconsin Ave
☎ 301/656-1500. 🖷 656-5045. $$

COLLEGE PARK, MD

Holiday Inn, 16.
10,000 Baltimore Blvd
☎ 301/345-6700. 🖷 441-4923. $

Quality Inn, 17. 7200 Baltimore Blvd
☎ 301/864-5820. 🖷 927-8634. $

ROCKVILLE, MD

Best Western, 3.
1251 W Montgomery Ave
☎ 301/424-4940. 🖷 424-1047. $

Doubletree Guest Suites, 4. 1750
Rockville Pike ☎ 301/468-1100.
🖷 468-0163. $$

Marriott Courtyard, 1.
2500 Research Blvd
☎ 301/670-6700. 🖷 670-9023. $

Quality Suites, 2. 3 Research Court
☎ 301/840-0200. 🖷 258-0160. $

SILVER SPRING, MD

Courtyard by Marriott, 15.
12521 Prosperity Dr
☎ 301/680-8500. 🖷 680-9232. $

Holiday Inn, 13. 8777 Georgia Ave
☎ 301/589-0800. 🖷 587-4791. $

Town Center Hotel, 14.
8727 Colesville Rd
☎ 301/589-5200. 🖷 588-6681. $

ALEXANDRIA, VA

Days Hotel, 55. 110 S Bragg St
☎ 703/354-4950. 🖷 354-4950. $

Doubletree Guest Suites, 56.
100 S Reynolds St ☎ 703/370-9600.
🖷 370-0467. $$

Econo Lodge, 53.
Rte 1 & Richmond Hwy
☎ 703/780-0300. 🖷 780-0842. $

Holiday Inn-Old Town, 52. 480 King St
☎ 703/549-6080. 🖷 684-6508. $$

Holiday Inn Suites, 50. 625 First St
☎ 703/548-6300. 🖷 548-8032. $

Morrison House, 51. 116 S Alfred St
☎ 703/838-8000. 🖷 684-6283. $$$$

Radisson Plaza, 54. 5000 Seminary Rd
☎ 703/845-1010. 🖷 845-7662. $$

Ramada Plaza Hotel, 49.
901 N Fairfax St
☎ 703/683-6000. 🖷 683-7597. $

ARLINGTON, VA

Arlington Hilton and Towers, 31.
950 N Stafford St
☎ 703/528-6000. 🖷 812-5127. $$

Doubletree Hotel, 39. 300 Army-Navy
Dr ☎ 703/416-4100. 🖷 416-4126. $$

Econo Lodge-Pentagon, 37.
5666 Columbia Pike ☎ 703/820-5600
🖷 379-7482. $

Embassy Suites, 40.
1300 Jefferson Davis Hwy
☎ 703/979-9799. 🖷 920-5947. $$

Holiday Inn-Airport, 41.
1489 Jefferson Davis Hwy
☎ 703/416-1600. 🖷 416-1615. $$

Holiday Inn-Arlington, 32.
4610 N. Fairfax
☎ 703/243-9800. 🖷 527-2677. $$$

Holiday Inn Westpark, 34.
1900 N Ft Meyer Dr
☎ 703/527-4814. 🖷 522-8864. $$

Howard Johnson's, 48.
2650 Jefferson Davis Hwy
☎ 703/684-7200. 🖷 684-3217. $

Hyatt Arlington, 35. 1325 Wilson Blvd
☎ 703/525-1234. 🖷 875-3393. $$$

Hyatt Regency, 47.
2799 Jefferson Davis Hwy
☎ 703/418-1234. 🖷 418-1289. $$$

Marriott-Crystal City, 45.
1999 Jefferson Davis Hwy
☎ 703/413-5500. 🖷 413-0192. $$$

Listed Alphabetically (cont.)

Marriott-Crystal Gateway, 42.
1700 Jefferson Davis Hwy
☎ 703/920-3230. ☏ 271-5212. $$$

Marriott-Key Bridge, 36. 1401 Lee Hwy
☎ 703/524-6400. ☏ 524-8964. $$$

National Airport Hilton, 46.
2399 Jefferson Davis Hwy
☎ 703/418-6800. ☏ 418-3763. $$$

Quality Inn, 33. 1200 N Courthouse Rd
☎ 703/524-4000. ☏ 522-6814. $

Ritz-Carlton Pentagon City, 43. 1250
S Hayes St ☎ 703/415-5000.
☏ 415-5061. $$$$

Sheraton Crystal, 44.
1800 Jefferson Davis Hwy
☎ 703/486-1111. ☏ 979-1708. $$

Sheraton National, 38.
900 S Orme St
☎ 703/521-1900. ☏ 521-0332. $$

DULLES INTERNATIONAL AIRPORT, VA

Hilton Washington Dulles, 20. 13869
Park Center Rd, Herndon
☎ 703/478-2900. ☏ 834-1996. $$

Holiday Inn Dulles, 18.
1000 Sully Rd, Sterling
☎ 703/471-7411. ☏ 471-7411. $

Hyatt Dulles, 19.
2300 Dulles Corner Blvd, Herndon
☎ 703/713-1234. ☏ 713-3410. $$

FALLS CHURCH, VA

**Comfort Inn-Washington
Gateway West, 30.** 6111 Arlington
Blvd ☎ 703/534-9100. ☏ 534-5589. $

Doubletree Guest Suites, 28.
7801 Leesburg Pike
☎ 703/893-1340. ☏ 749-8528. $

Quality Inn-Governor, 29.
6650 Arlington Blvd
☎ 703/532-8900. ☏ 532-7121. $

MCLEAN, VA

Best Western, 22. 8401 Westpark Dr
☎ 703/734-2800. ☏ 821-8872. $

Holiday Inn-Tysons Corner, 24.
1960 Chain Bridge Road
☎ 703/893-2100. ☏ 356-8218. $

**McLean Hilton at Tysons
Corner, 21.** 7920 Jones Branch
Dr ☎ 703/847-5000.
☏ 761-5100. $$

Ritz-Carlton Tysons Corner, 23.
1700 Tysons Blvd
☎ 703/506-4300. ☏ 506-2694. $$$$

VIENNA, VA

Embassy Suites, 26. 8517 Leesburg
Pike ☎ 703/883-0707.
☏ 883-0694. $$$

Marriott at Tysons Corner, 27. 8028
Leesburg Pike ☎ 703/734-3200.
☏ 734-5763. $$$

**Sheraton Premiere at Tysons
Corner, 25.** 8661 Leesburg Pike
☎ 703/448-1234. ☏ 893-8193. $$

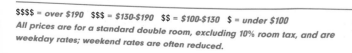

$$$$ = *over $190* $$$ = *$130-$190* $$ = *$100-$130* $ = *under $100*
*All prices are for a standard double room, excluding 10% room tax, and are
weekday rates; weekend rates are often reduced.*

MAP 54 Performing Arts

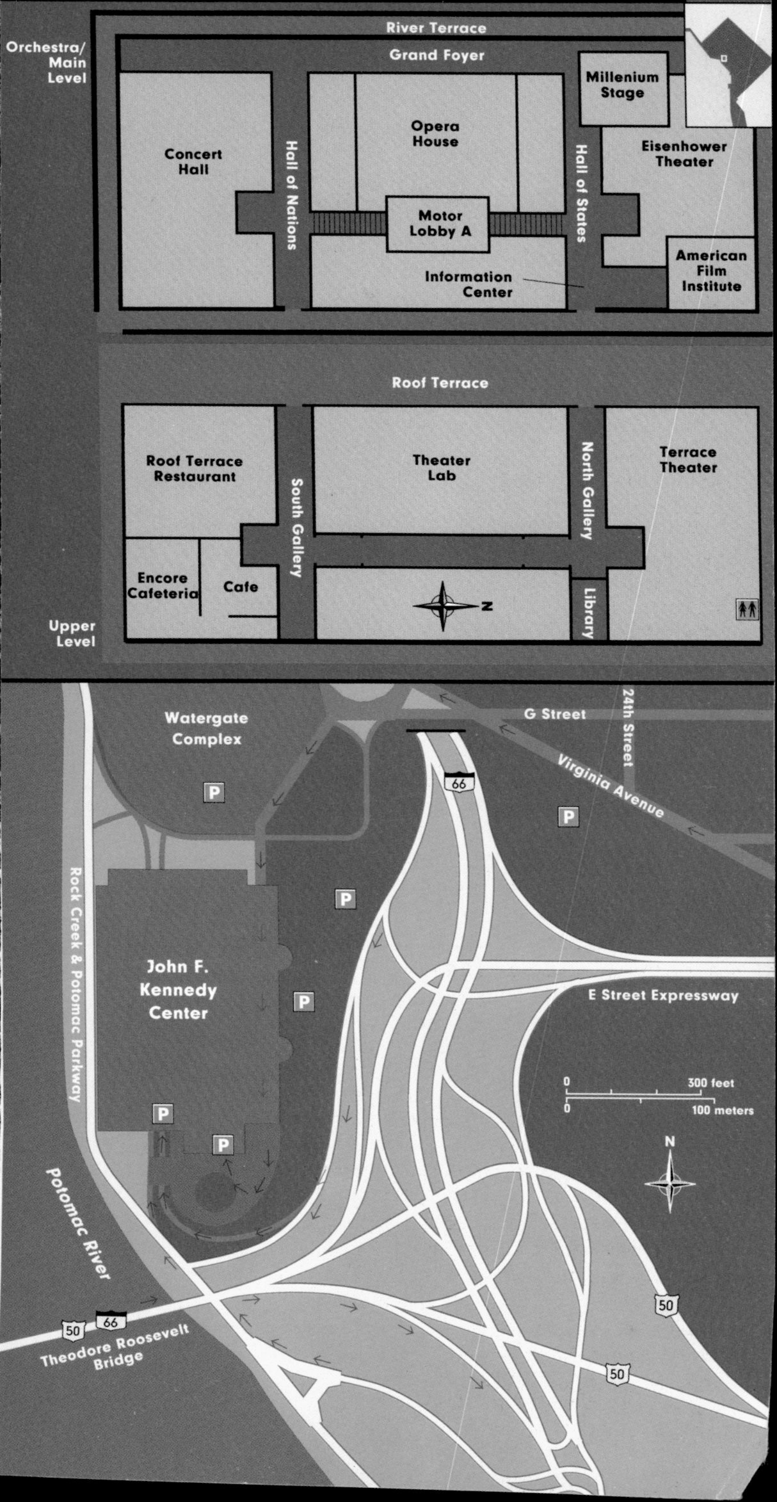

Kennedy Center

MAP 55

Orchestra/Main Level

River Terrace

Grand Foyer

Concert Hall

Hall of Nations

Opera House

Millenium Stage

Eisenhower Theater

Motor Lobby A

Hall of States

Information Center

American Film Institute

Upper Level

Roof Terrace

Roof Terrace Restaurant

South Gallery

Theater Lab

North Gallery

Terrace Theater

Encore Cafeteria

Cafe

Library

N

Watergate Complex

P

66

G Street

24th Street

Virginia Avenue

P

P

Rock Creek & Potomac Parkway

John F. Kennedy Center

P

P

E Street Expressway

P

P

0   300 feet

0   100 meters

N

Potomac River

50   66

Theodore Roosevelt Bridge

50

50

MAP 56 Movies

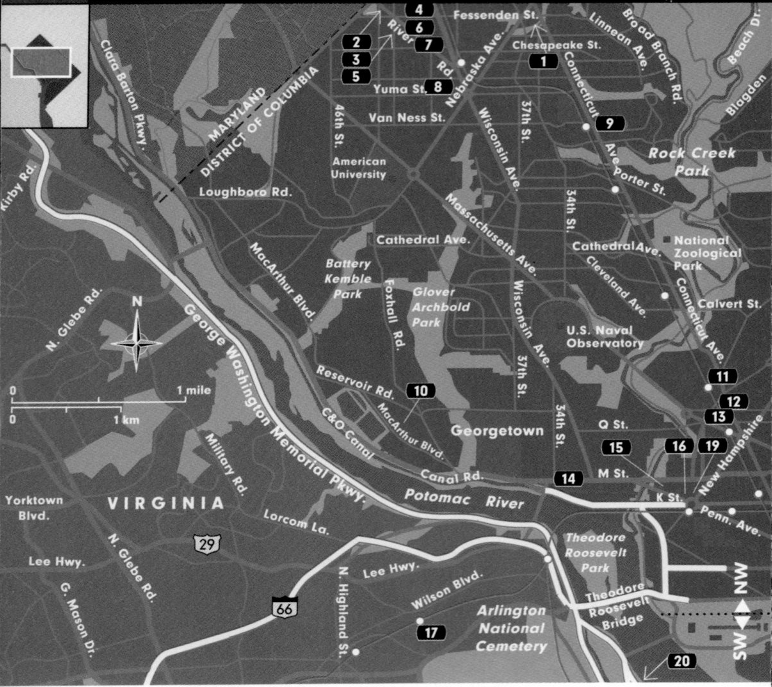

Listed by Site Number

1. Avalon
2. Paris
3. United Artists Bethesda
4. Cineplex Odeon Cinema
5. Outer Circle
6. Mazza Galerie
7. Tenley
8. Wisconsin
9. Uptown
10. MacArthur III
11. Janus III
12. Embassy
13. Dupont Circle V
14. Foundry

Listed Alphabetically

AMC Courthouse, 17.
2150 Clarendon Blvd, Arlington
☎ 703/998-4262

American Film Institute, 16.
Kennedy Center, 2700 F St NW
☎ 785-4600

Avalon, 1.
5612 Connecticut Ave NW
☎ 966-2600

Cineplex Odeon Cinema, 4.
5100 Wisconsin Ave NW ☎ 966-7248

Cineplex Odeon Dupont Circle V, 13.
1350 19th St NW ☎ 872-9555

Cineplex Odeon Embassy, 12.
1927 Florida Ave NW ☎ 387-1344

Cineplex Odeon Foundry, 14.
1055 Thomas Jefferson St NW
☎ 333-8613

Cineplex Odeon Janus III, 11.
1660 Connecticut Ave NW
☎ 265-9545

Cineplex Odeon MacArthur III, 10.
4859 MacArthur Blvd NW ☎ 337-1700

Cineplex Odeon Mazza Galerie, 6.
4600 Wisconsin Ave NW ☎ 364-8504

Cineplex Odeon Uptown, 9.
3426 Connecticut Ave NW
☎ 842-7773

Cineplex Odeon West End 1-4, 16.
L & 23rd Sts NW ☎ 293-3152

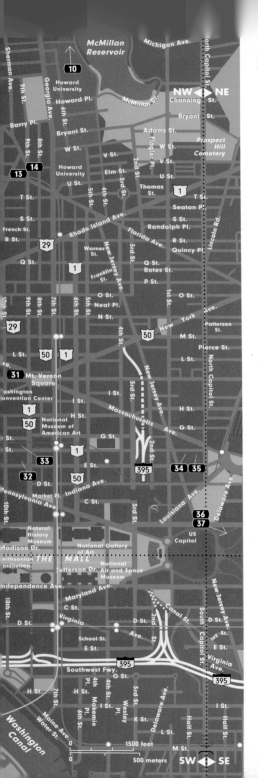

Listed Alphabetically

Afterwords, 22.
1517 Connecticut Ave NW
☎ 387–1462. Rock/Blues

Badlands, 18. 1432 22nd St NW
☎ 296–0505. Gay/Dance

The Ballroom, 37. 1015 Half St SE
☎ 554–1500. Rock/Alternative/Dance

The Bank, 33. 915 F St NW
☎ 393–3632. Dance

Birchmere, 38. 3701 Mt Vernon Ave
☎ 703/549–7500. Folk

Black Cat, 15. 1831 14th St NW
☎ 667–7960. Rock

Brasil Tropical, 20.
2519 Pennsylvania Ave NW
☎ 293–1773. Latin

Brickskeller, 17. 1523 22nd St NW
☎ 293–1885. Rock

Buffalo Billiards, 23. 1330 19th St NW
☎ 331–7665. Pool

Cafe Lautrec, 6. 2431 18th St NW
☎ 265–6436. Jazz

Chi-Cha Lounge, 11. 1624 U St NW
☎ 234–8400. Jazz/World Beat

Chief Ike's Mambo Room, 9.
1725 Columbia Rd NW
☎ 332–2211. R&B

City Blues Cafe, 3.
2651 Connecticut Ave NW
☎ 232–2300. Jazz

Club Heaven/Hell, 8. 2327 18th St
NW ☎ 667–4355. Dance

Dubliner, 35. 4 F St NW
☎ 737–3773. Folk

18th St Lounge, 25. 1212 18th St NW
☎ 466–3922. Acid Jazz

Food for Thought, 16.
1738 Connecticut Ave NW
☎ 797–1095. Folk

Grog & Tankard, 19.
2408 Wisconsin Ave NW
☎ 333–3114. Rock

Habana Village, 5. 1834 Columbia
Rd NW ☎ 462–6310. Latin

Headliners, 39. I-395 & Seminary Rd
☎ 703/379–4242. Comedy

Improv, 26. 1140 Connecticut Ave NW
☎ 296–7008. Comedy

Ireland's Four Provinces, 2.
3412 Connecticut Ave NW
☎ 244–0860. Folk

Irish Times, 34. 14 F St NW
☎ 543–5433. Folk

Madam's Organ, 7.
2461 18th St NW ☎ 667–5370.
Rock/Blues

Marley's Lounge, 31.
926 Massachusetts Ave NW
☎ 638–5200. Jazz

Marquee Cabaret, 4.
2500 Calvert St NW
☎ 745–1023. Comedy

Nanny O'Briens, 1.
3319 Connecticut Ave NW
☎ 686–9189. Folk

New Vegas Lounge, 24.
1415 P St NW ☎ 483–3971. Jazz/Blues

9:30 Club, 14. 815 V St NW
☎ 393–0930. Rock/Dance

One Step Down, 21.
2517 Pennsylvania Ave NW
☎ 331–8863. Jazz

Polly Esther's, 30. 605 12th St NW
☎ 737–1970. Disco

The Ritz/Decades, 32. 919 E St NW
☎ 638–2582. Dance

Spy Club, 28. 805 15th St NW
☎ 289–1779. Dance

State of the Union, 12. 1357 U St NW
☎ 588–8926. Dance

Takoma Station Tavern, 10.
6914 4th St NW ☎ 829–1999. Jazz

Tracks, 36. 1111 First St SE
☎ 488–3320. Dance

Velvet Lounge, 13. 915 U St NW
☎ 518–8944. Alternative/Dance

Zanzibar, 28. 1714 G St NW
☎ 842–4488. World Beat/Dance

Zei, 29. 1415 Zei Alley NW
☎ 842–2445. Dance

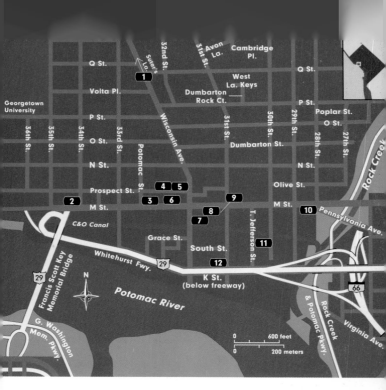

Notes

Hung Jury
1819 H St. NW
202-785-8181
(Farragut West or Foggy B.)

Washington Suite
~~2500~~ Penn

804

1900 W Monroe
62704

2370 Mass.

651-676-6481
Chuck Green

MnHS
345 W. Kellogg Blvd
St. Paul, NN 55102

3 forms of ID
& up to 3 references